GW00674272

FIGURES AROUND THE CRIB

Visit our web site at
WWW.ALBAHOUSE.ORG

or call 1-800-343-2522 (ALBA)
and request current catalog

Figures Around the Crib

Preparing for Christmas with
Isaiah, John the Baptizer, Joseph, and Mary

Reverend William F. Maestri

ALBA·HOUSE NEW·YORK
SOCIETY OF ST. PAUL, 2187 VICTORY BLVD., STATEN ISLAND, NEW YORK 10314

Library of Congress Cataloging-in-Publication Data

Maestri, William.
Figures around the crib: preparing for Christmas with Isaiah, John the Baptizer, Joseph, and Mary / William F. Maestri.
p. cm.
ISBN 0-8189-0902-1 (alk. paper)
1. Advent—Prayer-books and devotions—English. 2. Christmas—Prayer-books and devotions—English. 3. Catholic Church—Prayer-books and devotions—English. 4. Bible. O.T. Isaiah—Devotional literature. 5. Bible. N.T. Gospels—Devotional literature. I. Title.

BX2170.A4M29 2001
242'.33—dc21

2001022712

Nihil Obstat:
Reverend Denis J. Hayes, III
Censor Librorum

Imprimatur:
✠ Most Reverend Francis B. Schulte
Archbishop of New Orleans
December 4, 2000

The Nihil Obstat and Imprimatur are a declaration that a book or pamphlet is considered to be free from doctrinal or moral error. It is not implied that those who have granted the Nihil Obstat and Imprimatur agree with the contents, opinions or statements expressed.

Produced and designed in the United States of America by the Fathers and Brothers of the Society of St. Paul,
2187 Victory Boulevard, Staten Island, New York 10314-6603,
as part of their communications apostolate.

ISBN: 0-8189-0902-1

© Copyright 2001 by the Society of St. Paul

Printing Information:

Current Printing - first digit 1 2 3 4 5 6 7 8 9 10

Year of Current Printing - first year shown

2001 2002 2003 2004 2005 2006 2007 2008 2009 2010

Table of Contents

JOSEPH

MARY

Introduction

Why are we drawn to the crib? What is it that keeps us coming back to the stories of Jesus' birth? Regardless of age, station in life, and the firm resolution *not* to return to the stable, we find ourselves once again at the crib.

Why? For the same reason we find ourselves drawn to the foot of the cross on Good Friday. The eye of faith invites us to experience the unbounded, faithful love of God made visible. Such a love is a mystery which cannot be solved by our rationalism or cheapened by mere sentiment. The mystery of God's love is one that draws us in and lures us out of ourselves so that we might live for God and others.

Both crib and cross, each in its own way, invite us to hope. But it is the crib which offers us that hope in the *here and now*. The birth of the One in the crib speaks to our hearts of our own possible rebirth. The birth in that crib proclaims that one mystery and power which can liberate us for living a new way. And not just a new way of acting, but a real transformation of our inner being so that we might become a new creation. Such a transformation is possible when we open ourselves to the mystery of Divine Love.

The crib draws us because this transforming Divine Love never rejects the human. Our humanity is not canceled but revealed in all its possibilities. When the Word becomes flesh, the answer to the deepest riddles of human existence are revealed. The very question of our human existence is answered by the God who takes on our human face and embraces our full humanity. The question we ask about our lives is completely answered by God in the Gift of Jesus. And that answer is "LOVE following upon LOVE" (Jn 1:16). It is Divine Love meeting the human and conquering sin. Death does not have the last word. We need live in fear no longer. We can live free as the mature children of our heavenly Father. The dark night of guilt gives way to the bright star shining on the One who understands and accepts us.

To find our way to the crib is a journey at once short and intense. Advent is that gift of time and grace which calls for us to be alert. Without sound guides, we can easily lose our way or become distracted by some side venture. We are in need of guides who point the way and in various ways are present around the crib. For our journey this Advent, we surrender ourselves into the wise care of four who are present around the crib: the prophet Isaiah, the herald and baptist John, and Joseph and Mary entrusted with the earthly care of Jesus. Each in their own way will help us to find our way to the crib.

The format of our journey to the crib is straightforward and personal. Each day of Advent is directed by one of our guides to the crib. With the help of Scripture, reflection, meditation, and prayer, we draw closer to the One whose coming we watch for with patient hope. Each day is personal. In the unique giftedness of our lives, we come to see that the mystery of the crib does not lie in some distant land or different circumstances. We come to see how near at hand is the One who makes all things new. In the midst of our everyday, the Word continues to be born again so that we might be born anew.

I want to acknowledge my gratitude to the Society of Saint Paul and the community at Staten Island. Your ministry to evangelize is at the heart of the Church's commission from Jesus. I am thankful for sharing in this crucial ministry. Fathers Ignatius and Edmund continue to be inspirations for priestly ministry. Thank you.

I wish to thank Sheila McDonald of the Pepperdine Law

School who typed the entire manuscript. Your patience and cheerfulness were heroic.

For all who read this book and accept the invitation to journey to the crib, my thanks. More especially, may the One who draws us all with Love grant you freedom from fear and the power to serve Him in holiness all your days (Lk 1:74-75).

William F. Maestri
Notre Dame Seminary
Advent, 2001

"You have nothing to fear!
I come to proclaim good news to you —
tidings of great joy to be
shared by the whole people...
a savior has been born to you,
the Messiah and Lord." (Lk 2:10)

Biblical Abbreviations

OLD TESTAMENT

Genesis	Gn	Nehemiah	Ne	Baruch	Ba
Exodus	Ex	Tobit	Tb	Ezekiel	Ezk
Leviticus	Lv	Judith	Jdt	Daniel	Dn
Numbers	Nb	Esther	Est	Hosea	Ho
Deuteronomy	Dt	1 Maccabees	1 M	Joel	Jl
Joshua	Jos	2 Maccabees	2 M	Amos	Am
Judges	Jg	Job	Jb	Obadiah	Ob
Ruth	Rt	Psalms	Ps	Jonah	Jon
1 Samuel	1 S	Proverbs	Pr	Micah	Mi
2 Samuel	2 S	Ecclesiastes	Ec	Nahum	Na
1 Kings	1 K	Song of Songs	Sg	Habakkuk	Hab
2 Kings	2 K	Wisdom	Ws	Zephaniah	Zp
1 Chronicles	1 Ch	Sirach	Si	Haggai	Hg
2 Chronicles	2 Ch	Isaiah	Is	Malachi	Ml
Ezra	Ezr	Jeremiah	Jr	Zechariah	Zc
		Lamentations	Lm		

NEW TESTAMENT

Matthew	Mt	Ephesians	Eph	Hebrews	Heb
Mark	Mk	Philippians	Ph	James	Jm
Luke	Lk	Colossians	Col	1 Peter	1 P
John	Jn	1 Thessalonians	1 Th	2 Peter	2 P
Acts	Ac	2 Thessalonians	2 Th	1 John	1 Jn
Romans	Rm	1 Timothy	1 Tm	2 John	2 Jn
1 Corinthians	1 Cor	2 Timothy	2 Tm	3 John	3 Jn
2 Corinthians	2 Cor	Titus	Tt	Jude	Jude
Galatians	Gal	Philemon	Phm	Revelation	Rv

FIGURES AROUND THE CRIB

ISAIAH

So much of life is about preparation.

We prepare in our youth to take our place in the world, knowing each day is a preparation for that day when we will be received into the earth. Our hope is that like the grain of wheat we will bear much fruit in the Lord (Jn 12:24).

There are countless preparations, small and large, that dot our lives; from preparing for the big game, to the must-attend party, as well as the just-have-to-get-into school. We prepare for marriage and the blessings of our own families. We prepare for the birth of our children. It never quite becomes routine. And the cycle of preparation, anticipation, and realization continues down through the generations. We see ourselves in their struggles. We are renewed.

Advent is preparation. We are called to ready ourselves for the greatest event in human history — God becomes human in Jesus. World history and the human condition are never the same. The truth of both becomes revealed in the Word made flesh. The origin, meaning, and destiny of all are found in Jesus Christ. Preparation is required if we are to be drawn into this mystery that is too wonderful for us on our own.

Advent preparation requires participation by others. As we open the Advent season, we turn to the greatest of the prophets — Isaiah. His message is not frozen in time but echoes through the centuries to illuminate the meaning of Bethlehem. Isaiah speaks to us at the dawn of the third millennium.

The Lord must send a messenger to his people if they are to turn from their wickedness. Who will the Lord raise up? "Here I am," said Isaiah. "Send me!" And so it is that Isaiah comes to God's people in each time and place with the call to return to the covenant. God is offering reconciliation and peace. The challenge is to turn from the darkness which walls in God's wonderful light.

Advent is once again the time for Isaiah to speak to our hearts. We must listen carefully so as to understand. We are to look intently so as to grow in wisdom. We are to turn to the Lord so that our hearts may beat with joy in the Spirit. In so doing, the mystery of this graced season will bring forth the gifts of love, peace, joy, and hope (Is 6:9-10).

As Isaiah was sent to Yahweh's people in the second half of the 8th century B.C., so Isaiah comes to us in the 21st century with these words:

The people who walked in darkness
have seen a great light;
Upon those who dwell in the land
of gloom
a light has shone...
For a child is born to us, a son is
given to us;
upon his shoulder dominion rests (Is 9:1-5).

First Sunday of Advent

(Isaiah 6:1-13)

Holiness

The call of Isaiah in chapter 6 ranks as one of the most dramatic episodes in all of the Hebrew Scriptures. The very foundations of Israel's relationship with God are shaken. The covenant cannot be observed by offering sacrifice and grain. These serve as bribes in order to avoid the demands of justice and trusting totally in Yahweh. The covenant is not simply a vertical relationship with a god who can be bought off with some singing, dancing, and various cultic offerings. There is an essential low-zonal dimension which requires that Yahweh's people treat one another with kindness, compassion, and justice. Security is not found in economic power or military alliances. The sure foundation of God's people can only come from God himself.

A God Like No Other

Throughout Israel's encounter with Yahweh, one thing is clear: Yahweh is unique among the gods. The essence of God is holiness itself. The vision of Isaiah in the Temple makes this clear: "Holy, holy, holy is the Lord of hosts!" proclaimed the seraphim (Is 6:3). In the presence of God who is holy, Isaiah is filled with his own sense of sin and that of the people. "Woe is me, I am doomed! For I am a man of unclean lips, living among a people of unclean lips..." (Is 6:5). Isaiah can remain in the Lord's presence only after being purified by a hot ember. One of the seraphim touches Isaiah's mouth and declares him clean: "See, now that this has touched your lips, your wickedness is removed, your sin purged" (Is 6:7).

The holiness of Yahweh and the feeling of fear which grips

Isaiah prompts us to ask: What is this holiness of God? What is it that evokes a power to both fill us with dread ("woe is me") and at the same time draws us into its presence ("Here I am," Isaiah says. "Send me!")? To be in the presence of the Holy One is to be filled with a tension that almost pulls the prophet apart.

The tension between God who is holiness and human beings (even prophets) reveals the very heart of holiness: God is OTHER. Yahweh cannot be reduced to some force in nature, identified with a particular icon or location, and can never be controlled by cultic worship or sacrifice. Yahweh is above and beyond all that is. The other gods may seek after such things and be under the influence of the people. Not so with Yahweh. It is the Lord who rules in unapproachable light and directs all things by his mighty word. All the nations must acknowledge the Lordship of Yahweh. The vision of the prophet Daniel makes this clear:

Thrones were set up
and the Ancient One took his throne.
His clothing was snow bright....
His throne was flames of fire....
Thousands upon thousands were ministering to him,
and myriads upon myriads attended him (Dn 7:9-10).

A Holy People

Yahweh is not content to let heavenly hosts and earthly prophets proclaim his holiness. The Lord is much more demanding of his people. The book of Leviticus, the Book of Holiness, is constant in its message: "For I, the Lord, am your God; and you shall make and keep yourselves holy, because I am holy. You shall not make yourselves unclean.... Since I, the Lord, brought you up from the land of Egypt that I might be your God, you shall be holy, because I am holy" (Lv 11:44-45). To be in a covenant relationship with Yahweh requires that individually; and, as a people, we are holy as well.

The holiness of Yahweh is one which rejects a splendid isolation in heaven. The Lord's holiness finds its way into human history through Israel. God's holiness is for all the nations. And Israel will be the instrument by which all will come to dwell on the holy mountain of the Lord: "Nations shall walk by your light, and kings by your shining radiance.... None shall hurt or destroy on all my holy mountain, says the Lord" (Is 60:3; 65:25). Israel will reflect Yahweh's holiness by the way she worships and the way each member of the community shows love, compassion, mercy, and justice. By living the covenant, by being holy as Yahweh is HOLY, the nations of the earth come to recognize the Ruler of all the earth. The call to be holy has consequences far beyond geographical and political boundaries. Yahweh's holy will is being done through the covenant with Israel.

God Is With Us

The God who is holiness itself, the God who requires his people to be holy, is also the God who in the fullness of time reveals holiness in our midst. In the words of Isaiah, which find their way into the Gospel of Matthew (Mt 1:23), "For a child is born to us, a son is given us; upon his shoulder dominion rests... His dominion is vast and forever peaceful... The zeal of the Lord of hosts will do this" (Is 9:5-6). Holiness cannot be abstract or so far removed that we easily forget its call. Holiness will become particular, visible, and above all *human* in the One found in the crib.

Advent is that sacred time when the foundations of our everyday lives and spirituality, as well, are shaken. It is fitting that we began our journey to the crib with the figure of Isaiah and the call to holiness. For that is what our whole of life is about — growing in holiness as God is holy. Yes, we recognize our sinfulness which is ever before us (Ps 51). We are in need of purification which comes from the ember of divine love made visible in *this* child. And, yes, we are sent to sing out his goodness with our lives to all peoples.

Every great journey fills us with apprehension. Can we complete what we started? Will we know only failure? Let the words of Isaiah be ever before us as we make our pilgrimage to Bethlehem:

He gives strength to the fainting;
for the weak he makes vigor abound.
Though young men faint and grow weary,
and youths stagger and fall,
They that hope in the Lord will renew
their strength,
they will soar as with eagles' wings;
They will run and not grow weary,
walk and not grow faint (Is 40:29-31).

PRAYER

O Lord, you are the essence of holiness.
You call us to be holy so that
all peoples may walk by your light.
We are mindful of our sins and we
tremble in your presence.
We often lose our way as we
fashion idols which do not
give life.
We turn our backs on those in need
so the cries of the poor reach
your ears.
Your covenant is broken by our
sins.

Yet you will not abandon us. You
continue to send your prophets.
But now you are about to do a new
thing.

You come to us as one like us in the
Child who is Prince of Peace.
Let us not turn away in shame;
let our guilt be washed clean.

For you renew our strength
and in the birth of the
Savior we are born anew.

Reflection Questions

1. What images and experiences come to mind when you reflect on holiness? Can you relate to the experience of Isaiah? Why? Why not?
2. In what ways are you aware of your sinfulness? How has sin affected your growing in holiness?
3. How has God's purifying love touched your life? Has this experience(s) empowered you to tell others of God's serving love? If not, why? If so, in what specific ways have you witnessed to others?

Survivors

What do you say after a disaster? How do we speak to those who survive? What words of comfort and hope can be extended to those who remain to carry on? From the loss of life as well as the end of a friendship, we seek some words that will give meaning to the hurt, some acceptable purpose for our loss.

This difficult task often falls to the prophets of Yahweh. They are raised up by God to speak truth to power and challenge the people to turn from their wicked ways. If those who sit on thrones refuse to acknowledge the ultimate power of Yahweh, if those who preside at worship misuse liturgy to avoid justice and the needs of the poor, and if the people fashion idols, then destruction is near at hand. Again and again, the prophets call the people back to the covenant of holiness, a covenant of fidelity to the Lord and right living within the community. Time and again, the prophets of Yahweh are rejected and even killed. It is only after much suffering and death that the people are once again ready to return to the house of Yahweh. Before the prophet can speak a word of comfort, he must speak of impending judgment.

Judgment

Israel has broken the covenant with Yahweh by fashioning idols, seeking security in politico-military alliances, selecting corrupt leaders, and refusing to live justly with one another. The wages of such infidelity have now come to pass: the northern kingdom of Israel has fallen under the might of Assyria (722 B.C.) and Jerusalem witnessed the army of Sennacherib hem it in on all sides (701 B.C.). Just forty years earlier, Isaiah, in the year that Uzziah king of Judah died (742 B.C.), received his call to bring God's people back to the covenant. However, the leaders are weak; the people are easily led astray; and the pseudo-reforms only draw Israel and Judah into deeper destruction.

Unfortunately, the crisis which grips Israel and Judah will not be faced by the leaders. They insist on turning to the very things which are for their destruction — idols and reliance on political alliances for security. Every attempt at winning Yahweh back with sacrifices and liturgical celebrations rings hollow. There can be no substitute for doing justice. The words of the Lord through Isaiah are direct: "What care I for the number of your sacrifices? New moon and Sabbath, calling of assemblies... I cannot bear. Your new moons and festivals I detest;... Make justice your aim... hear the orphan's plea, defend the widow... Their land is full of idols; they worship the works of their hands... Jerusalem is crumbling, Judah is falling" (Is 1:11,14,16; 2:7; 3:8).

The crisis facing Israel and Judah is spiritual and moral not economic and political. True security is found in the covenant with Yahweh. Refusal to face this fact leads to defeat and exile. The Lord will use the enemies of Israel and Judah to inflict punishment: "He will give a signal to a far-off nation, and whistle to them from the ends of the earth.... Their roar is that of the lion... They growl and seize their prey; they carry it off and none will rescue it" (Is 5:26; 29).

The Remnant

In the midst of such gloom, one must ask: Is all lost? Will Yahweh leave his people to their sins and the destruction they deserve? In the words from Isaiah: "Rise up in splendor! Your light has come, the glory of the Lord shines upon you... Nations shall walk by your light, and kings by your shining radiance" (Is 60:1, 3). There will be a holy remnant, "survivors of Israel" (Is 4:2) and those "marked down for life in Jerusalem" (Is 4:3), that will return to once again continue the long pilgrimage to the birth of the Messiah.

The infidelity of the people will not provoke the ultimate anger of Yahweh. Israel is unfaithful; Yahweh is steadfast love. Israel chases after idols; Yahweh constantly lures his people back to himself. Israel searches for security in the love of power; Yahweh reveals that the power of his love alone saves. Israel ignores the poor and exploits the weak; Yahweh hears the cries of the poor and demands that Zion "be called city of justice, faithful city" (Is 1:26). Yahweh is the Lord of life and salvation, not death. Again and again, Yahweh's love creates "new heavens and a new earth; the things of the past shall not be remembered or come to mind" (Is 65:17).

Glad Tidings

Isaiah does not come with a message of cheap grace, that is, a restoration without reform, renewal without contribution, healing without conversion. Israel has violated the covenant in serious and protracted ways — idolatry, injustice, religious formalism, and trust in earthly promises rather than Yahweh's promises. Isaiah is direct in telling the nation what will happen — exile, and so it comes to pass. Yahweh's people is not above the law, but should be an example to the nations. God's punishment is the result of Israel's decision to abandon the covenant.

Yet Yahweh is the essence of faithful love. Chastisement leads to contrite hearts. And the Lord is ever ready to forgive and renew the covenant. God's purposes will not be thwarted by the waywardness of his wandering people. God's will is to be done so that the path will be straight, the valley filled in, the mountain leveled, the rough made smooth, so that "all mankind shall see the salvation of God" (Is 40:3).

The message of Isaiah is not confined to Israel but is for *all* the nations. Advent is a time of preparation not only for individual hearts and the Church but also for the nations: "The glory of the Lord shall be revealed, and all mankind shall see it together" (Is 40:5). Nations must search themselves and honestly face their commitment to justice, respect for life, concern for the poor, and stewardship for the earth which belongs to the Lord. There can be no security or peace without obedience to God's moral law. Freedom will become slavery if nations are blind to God's ways. Economic power is fool's gold when compared to the treasure that is God's law. Military might and technological advances only increase our anxiety and make war more likely.

At this moment in history, America dominates the nations of the earth. The temptation to arrogance is great and the challenge to humility seems absurd. Yet history teaches us that nations fall because their moral and spiritual foundations are ignored. Let us dare to hear the words of the prophet: "Put away your misdeeds... let us set things right... Make justice your aim... and you shall eat the good things of the Lord" (Is 1:16,18,19).

Prayer

O Lord, you are Ruler of all the nations.
Time and again we turn from you
and seek our security in idols.
We fashion for ourselves that which cannot
give life but only disappoint.
Our gold turns to rust. Our possessions
come to own us. Our power becomes
a source of our corruption.
We fail to hear the poor and defend the
widow and orphan.
Your anger blazes and we deserve your wrath.

Be more mindful of your mercy than the anger
which our sins deserve.

Let our sins of crimson red become white
as wool.
With a humble, contrite heart let us make
things right with you.

Our eyes are now clear to see those in need.
Our ears hear the pleas of the poor;
we come to defend the defenseless.
You are coming into our history to give
your peace to those who seek peace.
Make us an instrument of *your* peace.

Reflection Questions

1. In what ways has Israel violated the covenant? How do nations today ignore the rule of the Lord? Are they punished? How?
2. What are some of the most pressing justice issues that we face today? How has the Church responded to these issues? How have America and the other nations sought God's justice? In what areas must we show conversion?
3. In what ways has your faith done justice? How have you given prophetic witness by speaking truth to power?

Tuesday of Week One
(Isaiah 11:1-9)

Gifts

A sure sign of our present crisis in leadership is the number of books, tapes, and seminars promising effective leadership and quality organization. This present yearning for leadership is felt in society as well as in the churches. We desire men and women who can lead, that is, possess vision, display character, evidence competence, and promote the common good. Such leaders are at once born and made, the product of the times as well as possessing the ability to seize the moment.

Today we view leadership in terms of techniques, manipulation, and a "winning personality." There are a series of skills one learns and structures put in place which yield the optimum results. While there are certainly various strategies worth practicing and structures worth erecting, we must ask is there something *more* to leadership than techniques and pure organization?

The prophet Isaiah faced a time of crisis when it came to directing Israel. The rulers were often ineffectual, timid, and sought security in the very things (politico-military alliances) that would insure disaster. The religious leaders sought to bribe God with endless liturgical celebrations and cultic sacrifices. Religion became the people's attempt to avoid the weightier matters of justice. With a climate of such weakness and spiritual bankruptcy, it is no wonder that Israel and Judah suffered at the hands of their enemies.

Gifted Leaders

Isaiah makes it clear that leadership is more than good connections and noisy liturgical assemblies with huge animal sacrifices and cereal offerings. We moderns might as well know that good leadership is deeper than technique, manipulation, and the right organizational flow chart. True leadership requires one be open to the gifts of the Holy Spirit.

Isaiah details what Holy Spirit-guided leadership entails. First, such a leadership often comes from the *least* likely of places. In this case, Yahweh raised up a shoot from the stump of Jesse (Is 11:1). Of all places, the leader of Isaiah will come from one who is in exile in Babylon. God often chooses the weak and makes them strong in his service. Those who are far off will be selected to lead the exiles home.

Second, leadership requires that one be open to the gifts of the Holy Spirit. This infusion by the Spirit does not come from one's merit, intelligence, or moral worth. The gifts of wisdom, understanding, counsel, strength, knowledge, and fear of the Lord are bestowed according to Yahweh's mysterious design (Is 11:2-3).

Third, leadership must be guided in justice for all peoples, especially the poor. Upright leaders do not look at the externals of a person (riches, influence, beauty, popularity) but at their heart. The good leader is one who mirrors Yahweh's justice, compassion, and love for all peoples (Is 11:4-5). The wicked are punished (Is 11:4).

Finally, Yahweh raises up leaders who work for reconciliation. Divide and conquer are signs of the tyrant, not the leader of Yahweh. There is no room for the politics of resentment and the economics that divides peoples. *All* peoples are to be one on the Lord's mountain. The knowledge of God's ways will unite the natural world (the wolf and lamb will eat together) as well. All creation will be one in singing the Lord's goodness. Old enemies will become friends (Is 11:9).

Stump of Jesse

Who is this leader from the remnant in exile? Who will Yahweh send for reconciliation, peace, and new life? The Lord will send his only Son so that we might have life in abundance. The ultimate commitment of God to all humanity comes in the Incarnation. The stump of Jesse is Jesus who blossoms forth through the Holy Spirit. He is born in a manger in Bethlehem; filled with those gifts that release the power to preach the Kingdom; proclaims a time of favor to the poor; confronts power; and offers reconciliation to all especially the rejected, outcasts, poor, and those who believe they are enemies of God. Jesus fills the earth with the knowledge of the Father (Is 11:9).

Jesus is the ultimate gift of God to the entire human family. He is the human face of God's compassionate love. The justice of God is matched with his mercy. There is the offer of reconciliation and peace. On that Holy Night, heaven and earth join as one with the heavenly hosts in proclaiming that God's peace is in our midst: "There shall be no harm or ruin… for the earth shall be filled with knowledge of the Lord" (Is 11:9).

Advent Gifts

Advent is the time of our preparation for the ultimate gift of God — the Word made flesh (Jn 1:14). In order to receive this gift properly, we must ask what is the *truth* of the gift who is Jesus? The answer provided by Jesus is simple and profound: *service*. Authority is grounded in service, and leadership is expressed by being *for* others. Such an understanding of gifted leadership goes beyond technique and external structure to the very core of God's authority over us, and what is expected of us. Time and again, Jesus is in their midst as one who serves (Lk 22:24-30). This timeless and timely example of Jesus must always be front and center to the Church which struggles over "who is the greatest?" (Lk 22:24).

Advent affords us the time to reflect on our gifts and examine whether we offer them for the common good. Regardless of our social roles or status, we can be a stump of Jesse providing servant leadership to all who come under our influences. We can, in the words of the Apostle Paul, let our "attitude be that of Christ, who:

Though he was in the form of God
he did not deem equality with God
something to be grasped at.
Rather, he emptied himself
and took the form of a slave,
being born in the likeness of men." (Ph 2:5-7).

May his being born in our likeness transform us so that we may be like him in serving one another.

Prayer

O Lord, your gifts of the Spirit for every
time and season enrich
your Church and creation.
Let us not give in to pride or arrogance
but pour out ourselves in
loving service.
Let us think of others before ourselves.
Let our attitude be that of Jesus,
your ultimate Gift to us.

We pray for our leaders who bear
the burden of responsibility for
justice and the common good.
Let them be leaders in service
in imitation of Jesus.
Of special concern must be care
for the poor, the weak, and

the defenseless.
Such as these are dear to you.

Lord, during this holy season let
us each day give the gift
of ourselves to your glory.
Raise us up to be witnesses of
your gifts knowing that in
giving we receive.
In dying to ourselves, we
have the hope of eternal life.

Reflection Questions

1. In what ways have you experienced God's gifts? How have you shared these gifts with others? What has kept you from being generous with others?
2. How have you been of service to the poor, forgotten, and defenseless? How does such service relate to the Gospel of Jesus? The mission of the Church?
3. What are essential gifts for leadership in the Church? In society? In what ways can young people learn to be servant-leaders? How can such service prepare them for their vocation to the religious, married, or single life?

Wednesday of Week One
(Isaiah 25:6-10)

Mountains

On my first visit to Washington, D.C., I was overwhelmed by the number of monuments. From remembering presidents to honoring the dead who fell in battle, we humans have the need to honor those in the past who made our present possible. To forget is not only to be ungrateful to the giants on whose shoulders we stand, but it is also the reason we repeat the mistakes of the past. Our future then becomes one without hope. Monuments serve as reminders of who we are.

The Bible is filled with references to monuments often built by Israel's neighbors to honor their gods or rulers. Such cannot be the case with Israel: "I, the Lord, am your God, who brought you out of the land of Egypt… You shall not have other gods… You shall not carve idols for yourselves in the shape of anything in the sky above or in the waters… You shall not bow down… or worship them" (Dt 5:6-9). Anything which approaches an idol or image of the divine is rejected by Israel as a violation of the covenant. Too often monuments become symbols to human pride or attempts to confine the sacred to a particular place. Yahweh will have none of it. Yahweh is Lord of all.

God's Monuments

While the Bible warns against idols and monuments made by human hands, God has created monuments which draw all peoples to his banquet. The mountains serve as God's monuments. The mountains are part of God's good creation. They symbolize that which is strong, permanent, and beyond the everyday changing affairs of human history. To look up to the mountains is to be reminded of the One who formed them in the beginning (Gn 1:9-10). The mountain serves as the dwelling place of the Lord who is transcendent. The God of holiness dwells on his mountain surveying the actions of his people and all the nations. There is the hope that one day all the peoples of the earth will find their way to God's holy mountain. Zion will be covered with the multitudes that praise the glory of the Lord.

The symbol of the mountain plays a prominent role in the prophecy of Isaiah. The mountain of the Lord is a place of nourishment (Is 25:6), reconciliation (Is 25:7), life (Is 25:8), worship (Is 27:13), and salvation (Is 25:9). Zion will be the symbol of God's restoration of his people to their land and the defeat of Israel's enemies (Is 35:10). From the Lord's holy mountain, there will come that peace based on justice.

Throughout the book of Isaiah, the symbol of God's holy mountain as a place of salvation and peace is spoken of in the future tense. The mountain of Zion is a symbol of hope in the promises of God. The Lord who has been faithful in the past will also keep his promises in the future. God's people look to the mountains. Whence *will* their help come? The Lord's word is as firm and unmovable as the mountains. How long, oh Lord, how long?

Mountain to Manger

The God who dwells on his holy mountain now comes down to dwell among his people. The mountain of glad tidings will give way to a manger. The God who dwells in unapproachable light will be born into the darkness of sin with a light that gives life. The coming of the Lord into our flesh does not reduce God's divinity. The Incarnation restores the *truth* of our humanity and removes the veil which keeps us from seeing our authentic dignity.

Why such a reversal? Why does the Lord of the majestic mountain bring salvation to the poverty of a stable and the weakness of a child in a crib? The answer lies in the mystery of the God who is LOVE. God takes the initiative in closing the gap between the human and divine, sin and grace, fear and love, despair and hope. If God remains on his holy mountain, the depth of the divine love is never experienced. For salvation does not come at a cheap price. God comes into our all too human condition and forever commits himself to us. Henceforth, there can never be any doubt about God's unbounded love for each person.

God comes to us as a child so that we might grow up. The vulnerability of God teaches us that in weakness strength reaches perfection. We need not come to our God seeking salvation based on our moral merits or worldly achievements. The drive to earn salvation comes from our desire to boast. Ultimately, we want to make it on our own. Jesus becomes unnecessary. Salvation is not a gift but a right to which we are entitled.

Such an approach is futile and only adds to our anxiety. We must have the courage to let ourselves be drawn around the crib. For as the mountain of the Lord connects with the manger, so the crib will be one with the cross on that hill in which death is swallowed up in victory (1 Cor 15:54).

Prayer

O Lord, we lift our eyes to the mountain.
As with our ancestors in faith,
we wait for your deliverance
as we ponder your majesty.

Your holy mountain, Zion, proclaims your
glory. All the peoples of the earth must
find their way to your holy dwelling.
All the nations must recognize your
power and the justice of your rule.

Yet, we flounder in our pride and we
look to the works of our own hands.

Idols do not give life. Our monuments only
mock us.
Your faithful love becomes visible
in the Savior who becomes
like us so that we might grow into
the fullness of our humanity.

Lord, prepare our hearts for your coming.
Let us know the glad tidings
that ring out with the birth
of the One who is our peace.

Reflection Questions

1. What aspects of nature touch you about the majesty of God and the wonder of his creation? Why does nature have this power?
2. In what ways do you struggle with the seeming distance of God? How does the birth of the Messiah overcome this distance for you?
3. In what ways do you struggle with pride? Do you find yourself trying to earn God's love rather than accepting it as pure gift? How do the Advent and Christmas seasons help you humbly to accept God's gift of Salvation?

The City

During the time of Isaiah (the second half of the eighth century B.C.), it can rightfully be said of Israel, "You've come a long way." God's people is no longer a wandering band of tribes traveling in the desert as they recover from their harrowing experiences in Egypt. Israel is now a nation among the nations. She too has a king, and the people have settled into their own cities. On one level, life has become much easier, orderly, and predictable. At another level, life is more complex; and the passage from nomad to city dweller has brought a new set of challenges.

In many ways, Israel's transition to the city is filled with some of the same problems we face today. There is concern over housing, a certain loss of neighborliness and community, crime, and a general separation from those in authority with everyday concerns of the people. Also of concern is how Israel deals with powerful and aggressive neighbor nations whose gods and practices are unlike their own. International relations are more complex and call for an approach to politics that recognizes the "realities of power."

Even more pressing for Israel is the covenant relationship with Yahweh. Will the covenant change? Now that Israel is a nation, will Yahweh recognize this new situation and alter the relationship accordingly? No doubt some of the old ways must be left behind. Israel must now try and "fit in" with her neighbors. Such an accommodation is only natural if Israel is to get along with other peoples. Even Yahweh can appreciate the need to go along in order to get along. The ways of the desert must be left behind. The other nations must see that Israel is just as urban and sophisticated as they are.

Certainly, the new reality of being a nation and dwelling in cities must be considered. The covenant with Yahweh is not indifferent to the changing circumstances of history, culture, and human freedom. However, accommodation can never come at the cost of the essentials of the covenant. The quality of life in the cities of Israel and Judah depends on those aspects of the covenant which remain constant: fidelity to Yahweh, the refusal to worship idols, and the requirements of justice must be honored if peace is to be realized. These are the distinctive dimensions of Israel's covenant with Yahweh whether they dwell in the desert or the city.

The Glorious City

The image of the city has enjoyed a prominent place in human history. The philosopher Aristotle viewed the city as essential to growing in one's humanity. It was in the city that one cultivated one's intellect, acquired the virtues, and participated in those public affairs for the good of the life of the city. The Puritans who first came to America understood this nation as a "city on a hill" that would serve as a model of freedom, truth, justice, and the overall way God intended his people to live.

The prophet Isaiah is well aware of the darker side of being a nation with a complex city life. There is always the temptation to arrogance and pride. The people and their rulers forget the covenant and the need to follow the laws of the Lord. In being like the other nations, Israel can too easily forget what makes her special among the peoples of the earth. Greatness is not measured in terms of material abundance or politico-military security. The greatness of a nation and the splendor of its cities must be found in the moral well-being of the people.

Yahweh not only dwells on his holy mountain, Zion, but also among his people in the holy city of Jerusalem. The city must be a fitting place for God to dwell. Such a city must include far more than the "creature comforts of civilization"; there must be found justice and faith (Is 26:2), trust in Yahweh (Is 26:3), humility and care for the needy (Is 26:6-7), justice for all, especially the poor (Is 26:5-6), and a genuine desire for God among the people that inspires other nations and cultivates peace among the peoples of the earth. A city that lacks these basic elements may be rich and powerful according to the standards of the world but quite poor when it comes to its moral well-being. The soundness of a city is more than a standard of living which only measures housing, transportation, and communication. The sure foundation of a city, like the nation as a whole, must be built on the moral commands of God to do justice and live as a good neighbor to one another.

The City of God

Yahweh takes on a human face and is born in a city. In accordance with the prophecy of the Hebrew Scriptures: "And you, Bethlehem, land of Judah, are by no means least among the princes of Judah, since from you shall come a ruler who is to shepherd my people Israel" (Mi 5:1-2; 2 S 5:2). But the earthly powers have their own agenda. Rather than knowing the time of its visitation by God, the city is filled with people in obedience to the call for a general census by Caesar Augustus (Lk 2:1-5). Hence there is no room in the city for the Holy Family. The city is too crowded to find room for its Savior; too busy to welcome the One who is come for its peace.

God will not be deterred by human indifference. *Now* is the acceptable time; Bethlehem is the fitting place for the glory of the Lord to shine forth. It is not to the powerful, busy, or well-connected that the truth of that holy night in that holy city is revealed. The heavenly host's proclamation finds a receptive heart with the shepherds: "You have nothing to fear! I come to proclaim good news to you — tidings of great joy to be shared by the whole people. This day in David's city a savior has been born to you, the Messiah and Lord. Let this be a sign to you: in a manger you will find an infant wrapped in swaddling clothes" (Lk 2:10-12). In addition to the shepherds, foreigners from the east follow the star in order to worship the Messiah (Mt 2:1-11). The One for whom there is no room will take up residence with the poor, simple, and foreigners.

Advent is our time of preparation for the One who is and brings the good news. At this time of year we find ourselves more driven than driving; busy with many things, we easily overlook the One who really matters. The stars continue to point to the crib in Bethlehem. The heavenly host proclaim the birth of the Messiah. Shepherds still pause to listen. The wise continue to come from all quarters of the earth with their gifts. It must be that way with us. Above all, we must remember that *our* cities and small town communities contain those who are easily overlooked. Shepherds and foreigners continue to be with us pointing to the time of God's visitation. The needy, poor, homeless, and strangers are often more numerous at this time and more easily overlooked in our seasonal rush. Yet the least among us are gifts of Jesus in their need (Mt 25:31-46). It is a true city of God which finds room. It is a city that shall know a peace beyond all price.

Prayer

O Lord, we busy ourselves with many things.
You alone are our salvation.
Help us to order our lives in such
a way that we never look
past you. For all that we need
and hope to be comes from
your love.

To be centered in you calls for us to
be ever mindful of the poor
and welcoming of the stranger.

How often you come to us as
needy, homeless, imprisoned, sick,
lonely, powerless, and in
search of our love.
Grant us the wisdom to make
room in our lives for these. We
are making room for you.

As the time of your visitation draws
near, let us be attentive to
the star that shines and the heavenly
host who sing. They point us
to you.
And in finding our way to the crib
we come to experience that truth
and peace which we can only receive as GIFT.

Reflection Questions

1. What images come to mind when you think of the word city? In what ways can you help do God's work in the city?
2. Who are considered among the least of our brothers and sisters in today's modern city settings? How is the Church called to live the Gospel in the city? In what ways can you aid in this mission of the Church?
3. In what ways have you closed your heart to the needs of the poor, homeless, and powerless? In what concrete way can you renew your commitment to a faith that is active in love? How might you encourage others also to be more concerned for the poor?

Friday of Week One
(Isaiah 29:17-24)

On That Day

Not only place but also time figures prominently in the pages of Scripture. For God is not only the Lord of the mountain and city, but Yahweh is the Lord of history in whose hands is all of time (Ps 31:16). For the people of God, history is not some endless cycle of nature's birth, death, and rebirth. History is even less an eternal return or some cosmic wheel of reincarnation. Yahweh is the God who acts in history. The meaning and truth of the history are to be understood in light of God's providential designs. And Israel is the people the Lord has fashioned to be that light of truth to the nations.

The Day of The Lord

In times of distress as well as in times of prosperity, Israel looked forward to the day of the Lord. Such a time would be one of celebrating Yahweh's presence with his people and Israel's ultimate victory over the nations. It would be a time of visitation, liberation, and complete vindication of Israel's history. Often the great liturgies and sacrifices at the temple in Jerusalem were celebrations for the day of the Lord.

Yet there is a deep tension between desiring the day of the Lord and the *everyday* living of the people. Enter the prophets. Often those raised up by Yahweh to speak to the people challenged their longing for the day of the Lord. The prophets indicated that it would not be a time of celebration but one of condemnation. Why? Because the daily life of the people was such that true trust in God was absent along with a lack of caring for the poor. No amount of sacrifice or degree of elaborate liturgical celebration could substitute for rejecting idols and doing justice. The most powerful example of this call to do justice if the day of the Lord is to bring salvation is found in the prophecy of Amos: "Woe to those who yearn for the day of the Lord! What will this day of the Lord mean for you? Darkness and not light! I hate, I spurn your feasts... Away with your noisy songs! But if you would offer me holocausts, then let justice surge like water, and goodness like an unfailing stream" (Am 5:18,21,23).

The prophet Isaiah stands squarely within this prophetic tradition about the need for justice if sacrifice is to be acceptable to Yahweh. The dire predicament of Israel and Judah can be attributed to the people's infidelity. Idols have reappeared; security is sought in worldly alliances; and the cries of the poor reach the ears of Yahweh because no one among the people is doing justice. The day of the Lord is not one of vindication but judgment. Yahweh will use the pagan nations to bring punishment upon Israel and Judah.

Redemption

The message is not simply one of judgment and destruction. The prophets continue to speak in hope of a saving remnant that will prepare for the day of the Lord in spirit and truth. The force of Amos' condemnation still gives way to consolation: "But I will not destroy the house of Jacob completely, says the Lord... On that day I will raise up the fallen hut of David... and rebuild as in the days of old... I will bring about the restoration of my people Israel" (Am 9:8,11,14). Destruction gives way to restoration. The darkness has given way to the light of Yahweh's faithful love. God always works mightily so there remains a remnant to continue the covenant of salvation.

Again Isaiah is in that prophetic tradition of judgment and redemption. In the midst of a fierce denunciation of Israel's blindness and perversity, Isaiah seems to catch himself by remembering that Yahweh is the Lord of hope and life: "But a very little while, and Lebanon shall be changed into an orchard... On that day the deaf shall hear the words of a book; and out of gloom and darkness, the eyes of the blind shall see" (Is 29:17-18). The words of the prophet go on to present the Lord as a kind of understanding, supportive parent who loves his wayward children. Yes, they have sinned. The worship of idols, lack of trust and justice, cannot be denied. Yet Israel is still the beloved of Yahweh. God cannot forget his own. There will be a time of restoration and renewal for the people: "Now Jacob shall have nothing to be ashamed of... When children see the work of my hands in his midst, they shall keep my name holy.... Those who err in spirit shall acquire understanding, and those who find fault shall receive instruction" (Is 29:22-24). Throughout Israel's relationship with Yahweh, the Lord shows that his love is faithful even when his people are faithless. Salvation is the work of the Lord, and it will not be defeated.

In Our Day

What will the coming of the Christ Child be for us? A day of light? A day of darkness? What kind of faith will the Lord find when he visits us as a child in a crib? We know that the idols of power and destruction still abound. Too often we place our confidence in material possessions and techno-scientific wonders. We believe these will protect us and give life apart from the God who is life itself. Even in the midst of abundance, we know those who live without the basic necessities. In our rushing about, the poor become a blur if not downright invisible. Yet their needs are never far from God, and their cries are a judgment against our indifference. We are not immune from that prophetic judgment which demands that we do what the Lord requires — "Only to do the right and to love goodness, and to walk humbly with your God" (Mi 6:8).

The faithful love of God for Israel was revealed time and

again. Yes, there was judgment and punishment. But God's forgiving grace abounded more, and there was always a saving remnant. Hope, not despair, is the foundation of the prophet. God waits to visit us once again. The crib remains empty, waiting in patient hope to receive the Messiah. When the Word becomes flesh, when the day of the Lord dawns amid heavenly proclamations of peace to those of goodwill, may it be a time of grace and a gift of peace for us. May lifeless idols be smashed; the covenant of trust with God affirmed; and justice flow like mighty waters. In so doing the words of Isaiah and the birth of Jesus will be for us: "So he became their savior in their every affliction. He was not a messenger or an angel, but he himself who saved them… he redeemed them himself…" (Is 63:9).

Prayer

O Lord, all of our time is in your hands.
Your love guards our coming and going
during the day.
Your love grants us peace as we sleep,
secure in the knowledge that
your love rises before the sun.

It is in the mystery of time that you freely
enter our world and humanity.
You come to save us from sin and liberate
us to respond to your love.
Time and again we falter. We turn to idols.
We look to our power which is weak;
to our knowledge which is foolishness
in light of your wisdom.
We turn away from those in need.

Do not be angry with us.
Relent from your judgment.
Spare us the punishment we deserve.

Restore us by your steadfast love and cleanse
us with your mercy.
Then we can with hope await the coming of the dawn.
We can be eager to follow the star to
the crib, knowing we will not be put to shame.

Reflection Questions

1. In what ways are you using this time of Advent to prepare for the birth of the Messiah? Have you been able to find ways to join the Eucharist with care for the poor? How?
2. During the past year what idols have kept you from serving the living God? How do you plan to turn from these idols to the Messiah of Life? Has prayer been an important aspect of your Advent preparation for Jesus? How?
3. Have you felt God's judgment in recent times? Have you availed yourself of the Sacrament of Reconciliation? If not, what keeps you from the Sacrament? How can you overcome these obstacles for confession?

JOHN THE BAPTIZER

The excitement and anxiety becomes more intense as we pass from Isaiah to John the Baptizer. Yet much abides. Both figures are essential in our preparation for the birth of the Messiah. Both represent the prophetic tradition entrusted with preparing the people for the way of the Lord. Even though we leave Isaiah and his world of Israel in the second half of the eighth century B.C., we do not abandon his words. The shadow of Isaiah is indeed long and reaches to the "voice of one crying in the wilderness." In fact, the Baptizer is a *continuation* of the mission of Isaiah to turn the people from sin in order to receive the savior who "shall be called Wonderful Counselor, the Mighty God, the everlasting Father, the Prince of Peace" (Is 9:5). This connection between Isaiah and John is not meant to deny the uniqueness of John. It is rather to show that the Lord is not frozen in history but in each age prepares the hearts of the people for the Savior.

The world of John the Baptizer is one filled with suffering, resentment, and a combination of despair with hope. Israel during the time of John is occupied by the Romans and oppressed in deep ways by the Greek language and culture which Imperialist Rome spread as it conquered. Israel knew the might of the sword as well as the mightier influence of the pen (Greek culture). Israel also was filled with a *hope* that connects all the way back to an anonymous prophet called Deutero-Isaiah (or second

Isaiah). First Isaiah (an historical figure) spoke of judgment and punishment (Chapters 1-39). Second Isaiah (Chapters 40-55, the Book of the Consolation of Israel) moved beyond scolding to speak a word of comfort and hope: "Thus says the Lord: In a time of fear I answered you, on the day of salvation I help you, to restore the land…" (Is 49:8).

At the time of the Baptizer, the air is filled with the expectation that God is about to do a new thing. Oppression will give way to salvation. God is going to once again *act* on behalf of his people. The yoke of slavery will be broken and the reign of freedom, peace, and propriety will burst forth. God is going to act to *save* his people.

John the Baptizer appears at the Jordan River with a baptism of water and a message of fire. This is not a balm to bring comfort to the troubled, but a strong medicine that must trouble the comfortable. Life cannot continue as in the past. Old routines must be set aside so one can respond to the new things of the Lord. Above all, those who sit on mighty thrones and occupy seats of honor in the synagogue must do the unthinkable — repent!

If Yahweh is about to do a new thing, he certainly raised up an unexpected (and no doubt unwelcomed) prophet. But then since Sinai, the Israelites must have known this God was *not* one to play by the rules, especially the rules *we* make up.

(Luke 1:5-24)

The Man

"The man is found in the boy" certainly applies to John the Baptizer. The formative years of John reach their mature expression in his ministry *and* death as "the one crying in the wilderness."

When we want to find out about a person, especially one who is mysterious and carries an almost other-worldly aura, we naturally turn to their origins. Before we ask, "Who does he think he is anyway?" we usually ask, "Where did he come from? Who were his parents?" These questions are key if we are to come to some understanding of the last of the prophets chosen to prepare the way of the Lord.

Family of Origin

The Gospel of Matthew introduces John the Baptizer at the beginning of Chapter 3: "When John the Baptizer made his appearance as a preacher in the desert of Judea, this was his theme: 'Reform your lives! The reign of God is at hand'" (Mt 3:1-2). However, we are not content with such an abrupt entrance. We want to know more. We want to know about the background of the strange figure who identifies with Isaiah as "a herald's voice in the desert" (Mt 3:3). For some answers to one question about John's origin, we must turn to the Gospel of Luke.

The stripped down version of John's origin would read something like this: John was born to Zechariah of the priestly class of Abijah and his wife Elizabeth, a descendant of Aaron (Lk 1:5). Such a deconstructed announcement is at once factual and devoid of the most profound truth about who John is and what role he will play in salvation history. For completely missing is the remarkable story of life in the midst of barrenness; grace coming forth in what was thought to be sterile; and the advancement in age being no barrier to the plans of God. For God transcends all these barriers in order to accomplish his salvific plan. This miraculous conception to Elizabeth and Zechariah reveals the mystery and power of God to overcome what we humans believe to be possible. God is never contained by our limits or controlled by our expectations.

The angel of the Lord informs Zechariah that he and Elizabeth will be parents. The gift of this child is filled with "the spirit and power of Elijah, to turn the hearts of fathers to their children and the rebellious to the wisdom of the just, and to prepare for the Lord a people well-disposed" (Lk 1:17). All of Zechariah's objections are brushed aside. He is left mute because he doubted. His tongue will be loosed at the birth of his son who will be named John (Lk 1:13,59-66).

From the moment of conception, John is to have a special place in God's plan for salvation. The angel clearly indicates that this child "will be great in the eyes of the Lord" (Lk 1:15). Special care must be taken so that he "will never drink wine or strong drink" (Lk 1:15). The only spirit that will fill John is that of Elijah, the great prophet who will return to announce the Messiah. The spirit and power of Elijah will rest in John as the prophet who announces the "Lamb of God who takes away the sin of the world" (Jn 1:29). The reaction of the town to the birth of John indicates that God is at work. For there is a general feeling of awe and they ask, "What will this child be?" and, "Was not the hand of the Lord upon him?" (Lk 1:66).

The answers to these questions lie in the future. For now we must continue to look into the formative years of a child named John.

Into the Desert

It was bound to happen... with such an intense religious background, John was bound to find his way into the desert and away from the more mainline religious groups. And so John leaves the conventional and finds his way into the intense community of believers called the Essenes. They believed the end time was near; and, all those wishing to be saved should withdraw from the city and live a life of radical detachment, self-denial, and penance so when the Lord comes he will find *this* holy remnant. All that offers security, peace, and the well-traveled path of respectability must be rejected in light of the times. For God is very near. The non-essentials, anything but God, must be discarded. There is an urgency which requires we make a decision now! There is no later and more convenient hour.

It is in this desert setting that the words spoken about John at his conception are now confirmed. The word of the Lord is now addressed *to* John. He is about to embark on that ministry of preaching and baptizing which will lead to a confrontation with the religious and political leaders of his day. No matter. John's ministry is not the bidding of some earthly entity. The spirit and power of Elijah is about to be unleashed. "Even now the ax is laid to the root of the tree. Every tree that is not fruitful will be cut down and thrown into the fire" (Lk 3:9).

Our Own Desert

We, too, have the need to journey into the desert. The world is often too much with us, especially during this time of the year. The desert has its dangers: the unconventional; a vastness without demarcation; an aridity that gives rise to mirages; a home to beasts and Satan; and a seeming lifelessness that knows only death. Yet, each desert has its oasis. The flower blooms. In the vastness of the desert, we can empty ourselves so God's word can fill us up. We can experience that hunger which gives Satan an opening for materialism, power and popularity. We can know that satisfaction which comes to those who do not live by bread alone, refuse to bow down to earthly kingdoms, and put not God to the test but trust in his everlasting love.

Advent is *our* time in the desert. And like John, we are to emerge with the message, "Make ready the way of the Lord, clear him a straight path" (Lk 3:4).

Before we turn to John's message, we must try and take the measure of God's man who emerges from the desert. It is to the manner of John that we now turn.

Prayer

O Lord, before we are born,
you form us and call us
to do our part
in preparing the way of the Lord.
Our baptism in the Holy Spirit
makes us new creations
and members of your people.
Let us each day
build up your Body on earth
by courageously living the Gospel.

We must find our way to the desert
if we are to welcome
those temptations and demons
which keep us timid and afraid.
Send your bold Holy Spirit that we
might be those true heralds of
your coming in imitation of John.

The world looks strong
and its foundation unshakable.
The power of our hands
can seem invincible

yet all of this is but a breath
compared to your majesty.
However you challenge us to
not give into the love of power.
Rather we are to welcome the Messiah
who is the Power of Love.

Reflection Questions

1. Who were the major religious influences in your spiritual development? What concrete experiences were most helpful in forming your Christian identity? How has life in the Church been a blessing for your relationship with Jesus?
2. In what specific ways have you been a herald of the coming of the Messiah in your everyday life? What obstacles have you encountered? How have you tried to turn burdens to blessings?
3. Do you take time to be alone with Jesus in prayer? How do such periods of prayer help you prepare for the coming of the Messiah? What are those obstacles which keep you from prayer? How do you respond to those times when you find prayer difficult?

The Manner

One of the most powerful influences in contemporary life is telecommunications — the media. And in today's media-saturated culture, to borrow from the commercial, "image is everything." The visual has helped bring about a sensate culture in which everything is evaluated on the basis of the feelings, emotions, and first impressions that are produced. Part of the conventional wisdom of our sensate media-driven culture is, "you don't get a second chance to make a good first impression." That first impression is everything, especially when we are so easily "turned off" or bored. With a TV clicker in hand and an ever decreasing attention span, the pressure is on to get an initial favorable rating and "sound bite" your message. Anything over 30 seconds is sure to send viewers "surfing" for the next experience.

Leadership, religious and political, in a culture highly influenced by the media, comes under pressure to seek image over substance; a shallow voicing of opinion in place of serious reflection. Too often, there is the pressure to appear a certain way and couch the truth in a manner that appeals and doesn't risk offending a particular group or audience. Focus groups, media consultants, and public relations advisors surround leaders so the manner of presentation as well as the message finds a ready audience. And, when necessary, the leader is "made over" and the message "tailored" to provide a favorable rating.

Simply put: John the Baptist would never make it in our "image is everything" age where one's message must make people "feel good about themselves." John would be a media consultant's nightmare. He comes out of the desert "clothed in a garment of camel's hair, and wore a leather belt around his waist" (Mt 3:4). If clothes make the man, then this man is strange indeed. The very garb that he wears is a sign that something out of the ordinary is taking place. A definitive in-breaking of God in history is near at hand. For the very dress of John is similar to that of Elijah whose power and spirit Luke had identified as belonging to John (Lk 1:16-17). Matthew, after the transfiguration of Jesus on Mount Tabor, has John being identified with Elijah by Jesus (Mt 17:9-13). Elijah's coming will precede the arrival of the Messiah. Jesus tells the disciples "'that Elijah has already come, but they did not recognize him...' The disciples then realized that he had been speaking to them about John the Baptizer" (Mt 17:12,13)

If John's outfit is not mainstream, his diet would even test the taste of the most committed Californian! Matthew tells us that John's food was "grasshoppers and wild honey" (Mt 3:4). Why provide us with such a detail? John not only preached about the need to repent and prepare for the coming of the Messiah; John *lived* with integrity. He practiced what he preached. Even the most basic of enjoyments — a variety of foods — must be laid aside for the most essential need of the spirit — life with God. Only if we focus on the coming of the Messiah will we be found worthy of the kingdom of heaven which is at hand.

The dress and diet of John are perfectly consistent with his overall manner. That is, John is direct, honest, and uncompromising. There is no place for opinion polls, focus groups, or a therapeutic approach that is more comfortable with adjustment then conversion. The stakes are too high and the hour is late. Salvation by our God is near at hand. The ordinary niceties must be put aside. Clothing, food, and human respect must not blunt the radical nature of the need to repent. From the most basic of needs to the deepest of relationships, all must be understood in a new way with the coming of the Savior. For John, time is short. Decisions must be made now.

The Response

Our present day expectation would be that John is bound to be a failure. Audiences would be turned off by his strange dress and stark diet. His confrontational manner ensures that he will *not* win friends and influence people. After the initial curiosity wears off, the crowds will drift away and resume business as usual. Those in power who are the brunt of John's most severe reprimands can simply ignore him as a fanatic and a member of some fringe religious group. In time John, too, will pass away.

Our expectations, and the conventional wisdom of the well connected in John's day, are wrong. Matthew reports that, "at that time, Jerusalem, all Judea, and the whole region around the Jordan were going out to him. They were being baptized by him in the Jordan River as they confessed their sins" (Mt 3:5-6). Luke also reports that all kinds of people came to John — vast crowds, tax collectors, and even soldiers — in order to hear his message and be baptized. Furthermore, "the people were full of anticipation, wondering in their hearts whether John might be the Messiah" (Lk 3:15).

John for a Timid Time

Try as we might, we cannot and should not try to make John respectable so as to be more palatable to current sensibilities. John must remain his own man with a distinctive manner. This is not so much for John's sake as for our own. We need to recover our prophetic voice and preach the Gospel with uncompromising fidelity to the truth. Sentimental appeals and romantic notions of Christianity must give way to that hard mercy of genuine salvation. The coming of God in our humanity and history is the greatest of events. Decisions must be made. The peace of this season is the result of the Word becoming flesh and hearts repenting of sin. Conversion is not an optional lifestyle but the shaking of our foundations and giving some evidence we mean to reform (Mt 3:7).

The bold urgency and stark directness of John does not turn people away. Truth is the foundation of authentic freedom. Truth which guides freedom and is lived with integrity is an irresistible force. What turns people away is a voice which grows weak when confronting power. What is a scandal is not dress or diet but a compromise of the Gospel in the name of popularity or avoiding conflict. John knew it was peace*makers* and not peace*keepers* who witness to the kingdom. For making peace, unlike keeping peace which is really quietism and injustice, often means confrontation on the way to genuine reconciliation.

John as a man of God with a distinctive manner speaks to us across the centuries from the banks of the Jordan River. If we are unnerved by his person and manner, just wait until his message reaches our hearts. It is to that message we now turn.

Prayer

O Lord, each day you call us to go forth
with boldness and fidelity to preach
and live your saving Gospel.

Help us to find our voice so that we may
be faithful to your truth
and uncompromising
in speaking truth to power.
Help us to open our hearts to the Holy Spirit

so that we will not grow timid
or fearful in the face of opposition.

Each day inspire us
as you did the last of your prophets, John.
He spoke of your coming
and of the need to reform.
He did not fear rejection but knew
that the power of truth
would set hearts free.
He challenged all to give up old ways
and to be open to the God
who makes all things new.

O Lord, as you come ever nearer,
strengthen our resolve
and overcome our weakness with
your strong grace.
Let our daily lives be a testimony
to salvation and so draw others
to your amazing grace.

Reflection Questions

1. Which aspects of John the Baptizer leave you the most unsettled? Why? Which aspects of John do you find most essential to learning the Gospel? Why?
2. In what concrete ways have you been called on to preach God's truth? Did you encounter opposition? How did you respond?
3. Would John be able to carry on his ministry today? Where would opposition be found? What might John say to the churches of today? To those with secular power? The everyday Christian in the marketplace?

Monday of Week Two
(Matthew 3:1-3; John 1:29-34)

The Message

"The medium is the message," has become part of our taken-for-granted world. In the age of television, and the whole culture of telecommunications, the very medium influences what we see, hear, and how we process the information. In the very viewing and hearing, we are formed in various patterns of conversation, sight and sensitivity. We speak in short bites and have little patience with extended thought. We look for the image and the flashy, often failing to see the more subtle aspects of even a person. We become insensitive to violence, all the while demanding more stimulation in order not to become bored. In viewing the medium we become a certain kind of person.

With John the Baptizer, the medium is the message as well. There is a perfect fit between the man, his manner, and the message proclaimed. Even if his dress is strange and his diet stranger still, the crowds are able to discern that God is at work in this man. In fact, the externals are a source of attraction. Here is a man who shuns all the trappings of respectability in order to focus on what is most essential — the mission and message given him from the beginning by God. The Messiah is near. John must play his part. It is now time for the "herald's voice in the desert" to be heard; the crooked paths made straight; the valleys filled in; mountain and hill to be leveled; and the rough ways made smooth so that all the nations "shall see the salvation of God" (Lk 3:4-6).

Reform Your Lives!

With the suddenness of God's Spirit, John appears with the message, "Reform your lives! The reign of God is at hand" (Mt 3:3). The call to reform, conversion, is essential as the day of salvation is about to dawn. God is doing something new and people can no longer live in the same old ways. Even the most cherished of religious practices must give way to the reign of God. The old structures and securities must be perfected with the coming of the Messiah. Salvation has entered upon its definitive phase. The *active* reigning of God will be seen as never before. No longer will the Lord speak through the prophets. John is the last of these raised up to prepare hearts for salvation. From now on, God will speak through his only-begotten Son. John's demanding message is one which calls for a complete reorientation of one's life. This is not simply a change in perspective, lifestyle, or even values. There must be a conversion, a radical turn and return, to the Lord. The very core of one's being must be changed.

Yet we know that change is never easy. We resist. We find reasons to hold onto the comfortable and familiar. We rationalize the status-quo and even pretend that it is God's will that things remain the same. Very often we want to keep our power. We resist giving up control. Change fills us with anxiety as we must move to what is new and unknown. Just when we think we have things figured out and under control, along comes this Baptizer with his message of reform.

"You Brood of Vipers!"

Reform is not simply going through some ritual or external display of conversion. There must be a change of heart. The Pharisees and Sadducees came forward to receive John's baptism. John would have none of it: "You brood of vipers! Who told you to flee from the wrath to come? Give some evidence that you mean to reform" (Mt 3:7-8). This only served to infuriate the religious leaders who reminded John of their lofty status as the children of Abraham. John was not impressed and reminded them that "God can raise up children to Abraham from these very stones" (Mt 3:9). Religious status and natural birth are no longer sufficient for entrance into the kingdom. God's reign requires conversion and the inner transformation of one's being.

As long as there was no real cost involved, the Pharisees and Sadducees were willing to perform religious acts in order to be praised by others. John preaches that reform is not about human praise but God's glory. The Messiah is near. God's "winnowing-fan is in his hand. He will clear the threshing floor and gather his grain into the barn, but the chaff he will burn in unquenchable fire" (Mt 3:11). There must be a purification. Such an inner cleansing will be evidenced by the way one acts. Yet acts without inner conversion are worthless, and only serve to separate one further from God.

"What Ought We To Do?"

The talk of reform and conversion has an abstract quality about it which makes avoidance easy. Various people come to John and ask for specifics: "What ought we to do?" (Lk 3:10). The people want to know how to go about preparing for the Messiah. No doubt there is some kind of esoteric doctrine and secret teaching for the chosen few. Maybe those who will form the elect will have to follow John back into the desert. Surely there will be an agenda of rigorous ascetical practice and a grand display of one's commitment to conversion.

Once again, John does not live up to our expectations. After all, if what was required was a secret teaching and a demanding ascetical program, salvation would be for the few. There could be endless debate about what is required for genuine reform. In the end no one would change, and nothing would be done. But John will not fall for the trap. He responds with a concrete, specific message.

Following the tradition of the Hebrew Scriptures' emphasis on the importance of the particular, John tells the crowd, "Let the man with two coats give to him who has none. The man who has food should do the same" (Lk 3:11). To tax collectors who were much hated, John extends the call to repentance and membership in the kingdom. "Exact nothing over and above your fixed amount" (Lk 3:12). Even Roman soldiers can be included in the reign of God: "Don't bully anyone. Denounce no one falsely. Be content with your pay" (Lk 3:14).

John's call to conversion does *not* call for withdrawal from one's everyday world and responsibilities. It is precisely in the daily situation of one's life that repentance is to take place. The reign of God is within each person and is to be acknowledged in the routines of home, family, business, school, and the many occurrences which occupy our day. No one is outside the reign of God. No one is above the reign as well. Conversion requires charity, justice, truth and a willingness to serve the weak. Conversion is anything but abstract. John tells all with ears to hear — conversion is concrete; evidence of repentance specific; God's reign is among and within you.

As the Messiah draws near, we too ask John, "What ought we to do?" John's reply: "Give to those in need. The smallest act of kindness reveals God's love. Deal justly and mercifully with one another. Speak the truth so you will know peace. Don't judge yourselves and others by what you have. Riches of the Spirit are beyond price. Find peace in the everyday blessings of family, friends, graces, and crosses. Each day walk wet in your baptism and let the fire of the Spirit work through you to renew the face of the earth."

Prayer

O Lord, we hear the message of John to repent.
We find our way to the Jordan
but we hesitate.
The power of old ways
and familiar securities
keeps us from plunging into the waters.
We know such a baptism calls for us
to die to ourselves.
But we are afraid we shall not rise again.

We continually want conversion
without the cost of change.
We want baptism
but we don't want to go under the water.
We certainly do not want
to be touched by the Holy Spirit
who turns hearts of stone to flesh.

Yet we are strongly, powerfully drawn
to the waters.
We hesitate.
We want to turn back.
The power of yesterday is often stronger
than the hope of tomorrow,
with its unknown outcome.

However, we *do* know that tomorrow,
like yesterday and today,
is under your reign.
You do not call us to go alone.
As we rise from the waters,
we breathe your breath-life.
We are new creatures.
Help our weakness.

What are we to do?
Your prophet says:
love justice,
walk with humility,
do the truth with love.
Lord, we desire your coming.
Each day
help us to give proof of our longing.

Reflection Questions

1. In what concrete ways have you prepared for the birth of the Messiah? Are you able to share your talents with others through service? How?
2. What keeps you fearful of the radical change John calls for in preparation for the Messiah? How do you overcome these fears? What support do you receive from your local parish?
3. In what ways has the Holy Spirit inflamed you to witness to God's kingdom? How does God actively rule in your life? Be specific. What obstacles in the world and Church do you see opposing God's rule? How does God's kingdom overcome this opposition?

Identity

An all too familiar technique used to weaken or reject a message we don't like is to attack the messenger. We look for some character flaw. If we can find the feet of clay, then we need not take seriously what is being said and by whom it is being said. Maybe there is some hidden agenda in a message we find uncomfortable due to the messenger's ties to some special interest. Hence, the messenger is really the mouthpiece of a powerful group that has no concern for the common good. When the prophet Amos proclaimed the word of the Lord during the prosperous reign of King Jeroboam II (786-746 B.C.), the prophet was expelled from the center of worship at Bethel in Israel. His message was too much for the mighty to accept. Jeroboam enlisted the services of Amaziah, the priest of Bethel, to discredit Amos and banish him from preaching. Amos is accused of being a troublemaker from Judah who is simply being paid by those who are the enemies of the king. Worse still, Amos is branded as a "prophet for hire" who is simply preaching because he is paid. Amos will have none of it. He responds, "I was no prophet, nor have I belonged to a company of prophets; I was a shepherd and a dresser of sycamores. The Lord took me from following the flock, and said to me, go prophesy to my people Israel" (Am 7:14-15).

John the Baptist experiences the same treatment from those who are stung by his preaching. Personal attacks on John centered on his dress, diet, and desert experience. His clothes clearly indicated that he is outside the pale of normal people. Certainly religious leaders would never dress in such a way. His eating habits are held up to ridicule. Worst of all, he comes out of the desert no doubt brainwashed by those fanatical Essenes; no respectable prophet of Yahweh would come under their influence. His message and manner just go to show what we know all along: John is an intolerant radical with whom you cannot reason. However, like Amos, John will not be silenced. Yet questions about him do persist.

Questions

The religious authorities in Jerusalem sent priests and Levites to question John. What is it about this strange prophet who holds the people spellbound with his preaching? Why do they submit to his baptism? If we question him, we will discover his secret power as well as be able to find his weakness. The wolves in sheep's clothing find John and began their interrogatories.

The religious leaders want to know who John is. He answers in the negative, "I am not the Messiah" (Jn 1:20). They were hoping John would claim such a title so they could accuse him of blasphemy. No such luck. In trying to overcome this initial failure, they try to get John to say he is Elijah or even a lesser prophet. John answers in the negative. Frustrated, they demand some response from John: "Tell us who you are... What do you have to say for yourself?" (Jn 1:22). Again John refuses to play the game. His response is such that he does not put himself at the center but the Lord who is coming; he is the One John must proclaim. John is not the issue. Central to what is going on is what the Lord is doing and the need for the people to be ready for salvation.

The Pharisees have been watching with increased anger. The heat must be turned up. If John is going to play games about his identity, one thing he can't get around is his public activity at the Jordan River — baptizing the folks who came to the waters. If John is not the Messiah, or a prophet, then he should not be baptizing. Let's be direct, "Why do you baptize?" That ought to silence this troublemaker. That will put an end to his Jordan River following.

The surprising answer of John only adds to the mystery and increases the number of those to be baptized. John indicates he is administering a provisional, transitional baptism of water. His baptism will give way to the One who will baptize with fire and the Holy Spirit (Jn 1:26,33). John is laying the foundation for that baptism which will remove sin, overcome the sting of death, and restore right relationship with the Father in heaven. Such a baptism comes from the Messiah on whom the Holy Spirit will descend and from whom the Holy Spirit will be sent.

Give In For Now

The confrontation between John and the religious leaders from Jerusalem clearly indicates that John does not suffer an identity crisis. He knows who is, what his mission is, and he is faithful to the message entrusted to him. It is because he is clear about these three — identity, mission, and message — that John is able to recognize Jesus as the "Lamb of God who takes away the sin of the world" (Jn 1:29). Self-absorption, timidity, and lack of clarity prevent seeing Jesus as the Messiah. Jesus will face his three temptations in the desert. John faces his temptations at the Jordan River. Like Jesus, John remains faithful to the work given him to do by the Father. He knows his role in salvation history. He is clear about the message of repentance.

Day after day, John came to the Jordan to preach and baptize. The crowds were made up of repentant sinners, the curious, the hostile, the rich and poor, the famous, the infamous, and just ordinary folk. But this day would be different. The One who comes forward to be baptized is like no other. John simply declares, "I should be baptized by you, yet you come to me!" (Mt 3:14). The promises of old are about to be realized. The One who is to come is in the midst of God's people. Salvation is at hand. "This is my beloved Son. My favor rests on him" (Mt 3:17). John's acknowledgment of Jesus, as well as his need to be baptized by the beloved Son, is met with a simple, "Give in for now. We must do this if we would fulfill all of God's demands" (Mt 3:15). With the perfect, simple obedience of a true disciple we are told, "So John gave in" (Mt 3:15).

Advent is our time of preparation for the coming of the Messiah. We too are tempted to become self-absorbed in our many projects, timid in the face of opposition, and lacking focus in living our faith. John gives us the prime example of how to wait for the Lord. *Show up everyday* and remain faithful to who you are, your deepest commitments, and living the Gospel. What might have happened if John had decided to skip his regular work at the Jordan? He might have missed Jesus. Because he was faithful in his everyday commitments, John was there when Jesus came to be baptized. John didn't know the hour or the day. He did know the Messiah was coming. On that day at the Jordan, John was not disappointed.

Essential to discipline is obedience. John, like Mary, knew when it was time to be bold and when it was wise to submit to "God's demands." Such obedience is not a sign of weakness, immaturity, or passivity. Only those who are mature in love can know the wisdom of "giving in" to a deeper truth. John, like Jesus, is totally obedient to the will of the Father in heaven. This was not a sudden act or a spontaneous decision. John could "give in for now" because his whole life was one of "giving in" to the Lord out of love.

The Lord is near to you. The Messiah seeks you in the everydayness of your life. In imitation of John, show up and live your life to the full. In that everyday life, the Lamb of God comes. Give in so that all God's demands will be fulfilled.

Prayer

O Lord, your great gift to us is the Lamb
who takes away our sins.
We long for his coming.
We want to see his presence in our midst.
So often we become confused
about who we are
and to whom we belong.
The lure of the world and its fake gospel
so easily leads us astray.
In our confusion light our way.

We want to be a courageous herald of
glad tidings. We know that fear
can silence our voice and cause us to
seek security in human opinion.
Send your Holy Spirit that we might
tell of your victory to all the nations.
Let us show up each day and herald
your truth by the truth of our lives.

Our sins are before us. We are not worthy
of what you ask of us.
Help us to realize that your grace
is sufficient and completes
what is lacking in us.
Let us give in for now so that your
will may be done.

Time is short. Let the urgency of the hour
not fill us with dread or confusion.
Help us, O Lord,
to mark our days aright.
Let us turn to you, for we are never
disappointed.

Reflection Questions

1. In what ways have you experienced doubts about God's plan for your life? Why did such doubts come your way? How did you respond to these doubts?
2. How do you respond to opposition for living the Christian life? What part does prayer play in giving you strength and wisdom? When is the last time you faced such opposition? How did you respond?
3. Do you find it hard to be obedient to God's commands? What does the example of John the Baptizer teach you about obedience in God's plan of salvation? How do Mary and Jesus show obedience to the will of the Father?

(John 3:22-30)

End

The song "My Way" has by now become a musical standard as well as the anthem of an era — the culture of narcissism. The lyrics capture the spirit of the seventies; a spirit which has endured into the third millennium.

The song glorifies the rugged individual who faces the blows of life always on his own terms. The lonely, solitary individual, much like Camus' hero, who faces an absurd existence on sheer willpower alone, is much admired in American culture. Even when the anti-hero gets in over his head, he assumes responsibility and keeps on doing things his way. At the end of life when the curtain is about to ring down on our anti-hero, he takes satisfaction in soaking up as much experience as possible, always on his own terms. For this is what life is all about — experiencing as much as possible on one's own terms. Never give in. Always meet life head on and let the chips fall where they may. No need of raging against the dying of the light. No need to despair or become angry. The end of life is just that — the end. The only philosophy that makes sense is the one which counsels: Seize the moment, get all the experience and pleasure you can absorb. Have no regrets.

The Final Curtain

At first blush it may seem that "My Way" was meant for John the Baptizer. John was no respecter of men or public opinion. He rejected human respect and the trappings of respectability. John denounced the powerful and called them to repentance. John certainly endured his share of setbacks and hostile action by the religious establishment of his day. Yet John never compromised or tailored his message to please others. No one can doubt that John took the blows from religious and secular authorities. He was continually observed by the religious leaders as well as Roman officials who would not tolerate any challenge to Caesar's rule. It seemed that John bit off more than he could chew. Yet he faces the powerful with truth. John is thrown in jail, but it is his captors who are in bondage to sin and death. At some point the mighty will no longer tolerate this madman from the desert. He must be silenced. Even facing torture, imprisonment, and death, John still does things his way.

On the surface, that seems to be a fair reading of John and his ministry. But if we look deeper we find a wisdom and courage that indicates a different song is being played.

His Way

John the Baptist's entire life was one of doing it "His (God's) Way." That is, John as the voice crying in the wilderness never sought to promote himself or his own message. He is the classical prophet raised up by God to proclaim the word of *the Lord*. No temptation or threat or accusation can deter John from his ministry of preaching and baptizing with water. Because John is so secure in doing the will of the One who sent him, he does not look upon his ministry as a selfish possession or a badge of self-glory. John knows his time is short and his work part of a greater plan. John likens himself to the "groom's best man" who is filled with joy when he arrives for the wedding. Marriage is a sign of the coming of the Messiah. John has prepared the people for the royal wedding and banquet without end. He is at last able to say that the Groom has come and "my joy… is complete" (Jn 3:29).

John not only provides us with an authentic model of ministry at the Jordan River, he reveals what *all* ministry is about. In a final testament to his mission, John concludes, "He must increase while I must decrease" (Jn 3:30). These words capture the essence of ministry, mission, and message: Jesus must be the One we proclaim; the One we serve; and the One whom we bring to the world. The temptation is to increase in our own self-estimation. We fall victim to flattery, pride, and, worst of all, ambition for status. This is a ministry devoted to self rather than Jesus, Church, and others. This is the ministry of "My Way." Such labors end in disillusionment and failure. It is only when we grow less, when we let Jesus increase, that we know a joy the world cannot give or take away. We are doing ministry "His Way."

The Final Curtain

With the passage of time, our capacities decrease. True to the lyrics of the song "My Way," we all face the final curtain. The time for John's dissolution is near. He has fought the good fight; run the race; kept the faith; and proclaimed the Word in season and out, convenient or inconvenient. But he faces the end not with the resignation of the Stoic or the indifference of some contemporary character who refuses to hope. John does not come to the final curtain with a false bravado and a mask of revelry as a way of hiding the anxiety. John faces the final curtain as a man of faith. He can grow less because Jesus' becoming more is John's hope for salvation. John's faith is not some mindless leap into the unknown; a blind jump into the irrational. John's faith is one guided by the light of truth, namely the God who makes promises and keeps promises. God never goes back on his word or abandons those whom he chooses.

The greatest proof of God's fidelity is the coming of the Bridegroom. Already the guests are coming — poor, blind, lame, sinners, publicans, widows and orphans. Even before the Jordan River, the child in the crib was drawing angels, shepherds, and wise men. The opening act in Bethlehem and the final curtain on Golgotha unite to tell the greatest story of God's love, and the divine invitation to faith, hope and love.

John the Baptizer's work is complete. The baptism of water must pass into the baptism of fire. The end for John is near. The forces of darkness are about to make their move. The world will have its way with this troublesome voice from the desert. In the tradition of all the great prophets, John is about to be handed over to the forces of death.

Yet because of the crib and the One who lives, the end is about the ultimate beginning. It is to John's new beginning that we now turn.

Prayer

O Lord, you know how much we desire to
do things our way.
We are self-absorbed and turn from you
and the needs of those around us.
We suffer from that pride which
rebels against your truth and
causes us to serve ourselves rather
than acknowledge your gifts.

Help us to learn from your faithful
herald, John the Baptizer.
Let us place Jesus, the Bridegroom,
at the center of our lives.
Let us do his will and not ours;
show forth his goodness and
not seek our glory.
In so doing we know that joy in
the Holy Spirit which is but
a foretaste of your love for us.

The realization that we must grow less
fills us with fear.
Who will provide for us?
Who will save us from the dying of

the light? Where will help come
as the final curtain comes down
on our lives?

Lord, help us to look to the crib
and know you never abandon us.
Your salvation is that gift
which overcomes the terror of the night.
In doing your thing, your way, we truly live.

Reflection Questions

1. Why do you find yourself doing things your way instead of God's way? In what areas of your life is this especially true? Of what are you afraid?
2. What aspects of John's ministry has most influenced you? Are you able to put these qualities into practice? If not, what are the major obstacles?
3. In what ways has God been faithful to you? How have you responded to God's fidelity? How does your preparation for the birth of the Messiah help you live more faithfully the Christian life? Be specific.

Thursday of Week Two
(Matthew 11:2-5; Mark 6:14-29)

The Beginning

It was just a matter of time before the powers of this passing world would employ their ultimate weapon against John — the power to arrest, jail, and kill God's herald of the Messiah. Of course this ultimate weapon exposes the world's ultimate weakness. God's word will not be silenced. God continues to raise up men and women to proclaim the truth. What the world understands as the end is in reality the beginning. Yes, John will be removed from the Jordan River. The crowds will follow Another. The attention of the authorities will shift to new flashpoints of controversy. But at least the mighty will be rid of this fanatic and his intolerable message. Or will they? Will John's confinement be in reality authentic liberation? Will John the Baptizer's death be that passage into eternal life? The answer to these questions is the rest of the story.

An Old Score to Settle

John the Baptizer was at the top of Herodias' enemies list. She was married to Herod, the brother of her first husband Philip. The Levitical law does not allow such a marriage (Lv 18:16). John confronted Herod and Herodias and called for them to end their scandalous relationship. This public call to repentance sealed John's fate: "Herodias harbored a grudge against him for this and wanted to kill him..." (Mk 6:19). However, this was not possible initially because so many of the people considered John a true prophet. As usual, the people were ahead of the leaders. For now Herodias had to settle for John's imprisonment. She wanted John to be killed; but Herod, who was weak morally, believed John was a holy man from God and found his preaching both disturbing and attractive. Weakness always seeks compromise which only brings about greater conflict. Hence, Herod ordered John to be "arrested, chained, and imprisoned..." (Mk 6:17).

This cowardly response by Herod (similar to Pilate's having Jesus scourged and crowned with thorns) only encourages Herodias to find a way to kill John. The moral weakness of the worldly strong is often vain-glory or pride. Hence, at a party Herod is "delighted" at a dance performed by Herodias' daughter. The beautiful people as well as the power brokers are all in attendance. Herod is so filled with pride (and lust) that he swears publicly to the girl, "Ask for anything you want and I will give it to you" (Mk 6:22). After consulting with her mother, the not-so-surprising answer comes, "I want you to give me, at once, the head of John the Baptizer on a platter" (Mk 6:25).

In a show of vice masquerading as virtue, Herod feels the need to keep his oath. It would be giving bad example to go back on one's word. The people expect their leaders to set the right moral tone. Indeed. It is really Herod's pride that motivates him to fulfill this murderous request. And so the Baptizer is beheaded and the trophy is presented to Herodias. It seems as if you wait long enough, vengeance can be enacted. John's disciples come and take the body away for burial (Mk 6:29).

Request From Prison

Some of the best writing and reflection comes from a sick bed or a prison cell. These have a way of focusing our attention on the things that really matter. Between John's arrest and martyrdom, he managed to do a great deal of reflecting on his life and mission. No doubt he had to confront the nagging questions that plague the confined who give up so much: Was the cost too much? Where is God to be found in this situation? Did I do everything that was expected? In the end will I be saved and the

Lord's truth endure? These and many other questions turned over in John's mind as a human being.

In Matthew's Gospel we read of his imprisonment and gain an insight into the humanity of this man named John. John has decreased and the fame of Jesus is increasing as his teaching and works become more wondrous. John must know... is Jesus *really* the One who is to come? (Mt 11:3).

Such a human request at the end of his life's work. John needs to know from Jesus himself if he is the Messiah. Yes, John baptized Jesus at the Jordan. Yes, John declared Jesus to be the Lamb who takes away sin and baptizes with fire. But now in prison John must know *from* Jesus. John gets word to Jesus by way of his own disciples: "Are you 'He who is to come' or do we look for another?" (Mt 11:3).

Jesus responds in the most powerful of ways; namely, he instructs John's disciples to be witnesses of what they see and hear: "The blind recover their sight, cripples walk, lepers are cured, the deaf hear, dead men are raised to life, and the poor have the good news preached to them. Blest is the man who finds no stumbling block in me" (Mt 11:5-6). All of these signs are definitive expressions of the Kingdom of God. To the eye of faith there can be no doubt as to who Jesus is — "He who is to come." Jesus is a stumbling block, scandal, and rejected cornerstone as well as the source of joy which comes with God's salvation through the Messiah.

Jesus' Witness to John

The tables are turned. John, whose whole life has been one of witness and proclamation, will now be proclaimed by Jesus. To be sure, John did not meet the expectations of the crowds and the authorities. He was not "a reed swaying in the wind." John spoke the truth of God with courage and never concerned himself with human opinion. Unlike those leaders who seek security in numbers, John's only concern was fidelity to his mission of calling the people to repent for the Messiah was near. Even less was John dressed luxuriously and found in royal palaces. John was poor so God could be rich in him. John was powerless so God's saving power could turn hearts to the Messiah.

John was not a prophet. He was *more* than a prophet. John is the messenger sent by the Father to prepare the people for Jesus (Mt 11:10). More powerful still, Jesus understands John in terms of Elijah, the one whose return signals the coming of the Messiah. "If you are prepared to accept it, he is Elijah, the one who was certain to come. Heed carefully what you hear!" (Mt 11:14). For if you acknowledge the role of John in light of Elijah, then you must take the responsibility for accepting or rejecting his voice; for acknowledging or denying Jesus as the Messiah. There is no middle ground or compromise. With John and Jesus, those who hear and see are called to make a decision for which one must accept complete responsibility.

Blessed will *we* be if we find no stumbling block in them.

PRAYER

O Lord, in being faithful to your word
and committed to your work,
we find ourselves surrounded by foes.
We are tempted to retreat
and abandon your call.
We are in need of your saving grace.

At times we are surrounded
by inner fears and uncertainties.
We doubt our resolve to do your will.
We are assailed by the thoughts
of our own unworthiness.

We tremble when we consider
what you expect of us.

We are imprisoned by our weakness.
Let your Holy Spirit
work through our weakness
that you might be strong
through us.
Like John, we must know
if Jesus is the One.

Let us see your wonders;
let us be cured of our infirmities;
let us rise to new life;
let us hear the good news;
and in our poverty
may we be rich in your love.

Above all, Lord,
let us not find a stumbling block in you.
Rather,
let us find you in the crib
so that
we might grow up in that faith
which leads to eternal life.

Reflection Questions

1. What hardships have you recently experienced in witnessing to the Messiah? How have you responded? In what specific ways has God's grace been your strength and shield?
2. What doubts do you struggle with when you reflect on God's presence? In what ways have prayer and the sacraments been a source of strength? In what areas of your relationship with Jesus do you experience the most doubts? How do you find inner peace?

3. Are there aspects of Jesus' life that you experience as a stumbling block? Why? Do you experience support for your faith from your local church? How? What might you do to strengthen your local faith community in preparation for the birth of the Messiah?

JOSEPH

We need a break! We must take time to catch our spiritual second wind as we wind our way through Advent. The season is short but intense. If we hope to arrive in Bethlehem and be found around the crib on Christmas morning, we must learn to pace ourselves. We don't want to be like some flashy star that burns brightly but quickly fades. Our hope is to be like that steady star over Bethlehem which provided a sure light to the One who is the Light of the world.

The past two weeks with Isaiah and John the Baptizer have been demanding. Each received dramatic calls to proclaim Yahweh's word to hearts turned to stone and in need of conversion. Each faced strong opposition. The mighty were not used to having truth spoken to their power. Each, in their own time and place, pointed to the One born in Bethlehem. Isaiah and John played essential roles in preparing the way of the Lord. In fact, John identifies himself using the words of Isaiah: "A herald's voice in the desert: 'Prepare the way of the Lord, make straight his paths'" (Mt 3:3).

Isaiah and the Baptizer, our two preparation figures around the crib, are in place. We now turn our attention to one who is described in the genealogy of Jesus simply as "Joseph, the husband of Mary" (Mt 1:16). Throughout the Gospels of Matthew and Luke, the simplest of descriptions will be used to describe

Joseph. Such underplaying may in reality be a way of calling our attention to the saving presence of God in this uncommon common man.

Our contemporary mentality toward those in public life is to delve into their past and find the flaw. The "tabloidization" of biography is done in the name of honesty, reality, and truth. Yet in truth we chip away at our heroes and whittle down our leaders. In the process *we* become less ourselves. Without the shoulders of giants to stand on, we cannot look very far into the future. Our horizon is small, and our capacity to hope is less than our willingness to despair. We become cynical and disillusioned.

There is a sparseness about Joseph that frustrates the current rage to get at the historical figure; the "historical Joseph." The gospel writers do not define Joseph as much as they describe him in pithy episodes of action which give insight into his character and faith. Joseph is not to be limited by definitions. The complex and profound often come in simple, direct ways. We must lay aside our present day prejudice for unearthing tidbits of scandal. Only in so doing will we come to see the holiness and strength of "Mary's husband." We will come to see how indispensable Joseph is for our pilgrimage to the crib.

To this Everyman of ordinary appearance we now turn, in hopes of seeing the ways of God's extraordinary grace.

The Quiet Man

Too often the morally upright appear to be uptight. This takes all the joy out of living a virtuous life. Yes, there is joy in living the virtues and growing in our humanity. There is an overwhelming joy in the Holy Spirit through the infused virtues of faith, hope, and charity. And yet, so often the joy is missing. We come across as gloomy saints who need to look more redeemed. Yet with the messages — "a savior has been born to you, the Messiah and Lord" in addition to "He is not here; he has been raised up" — joy, happiness, and peace are our inheritance. We must not confuse scolding, finger waving, and frowning with the moral life. Inner transformation does not come from external pressure. Yes, we can get people to change their behavior, but conversion of the heart is the work of grace. And it is our hearts, our whole being, which the Messiah transforms by love. Conversion without action is sentiment. Action without conversion is formalism. A heartfelt work of love is the authentic fruit of the Holy Spirit.

An Upright Man

Today, there is much confusion about what it means to be a real man and a real woman. The proof of such confusion is the sheer volume of books, tapes, articles, and seminars on *how* to be a man or a woman. It seems that the old role expectations no longer apply. From holding a door to offering a compliment, the rules have changed. Women try to tell men what is important and what they want. Men are frustrated by what they perceive to be a rejection of their presence as important for love and family. The insecurity among men grows more pronounced as women continue to claim that "men just don't get it." Men might well agree, although the *cause* for not getting it would certainly be debated.

Why not look to Joseph? For there is about him an inner strength that is at once admirable, strong, and understanding for those in difficult circumstances. Joseph is not a sentimental romantic who confuses apathy with tolerance, moral laxity with understanding. Joseph is secure enough in his identity that he does not turn to vengeance to prop up a sagging ego. Joseph does not claim his rights because he is more interested in doing the right thing.

We first meet Joseph in a rather awkward situation to say the least. His intended wife, Mary, was "found with child." They were not married, and Joseph knew he was not the father. What to do? Surprise, hurt, and anger all seem like quite normal reactions to the situation. No doubt Joseph felt these. However, he is not a man driven by emotion but by a desire to do what is right. The Mosaic law is clearly on his side. Joseph could publicly expose Mary as an adulteress, and let her suffer the consequences that would result from such a disclosure. Why not? After all, he is the victim! He has been wronged, and Mary must satisfy the injustice. Also, Joseph will experience a great deal of embarrassment. How to explain the situation to family and friends? Joseph is human and his male ego has been hurt. The law will be applied and satisfaction made for this sin.

Sometimes we catch a glimpse of a person by what they *don't* do rather than by what they do. Joseph will not press his legal rights. Joseph will not expose Mary, nor claim paternity for this child. In this we see that Joseph is not driven by vengeance or the need to save face. He is "an upright man." As a man of God, he must balance truth (he is not the father) with love (he will not expose Mary to the law). Joseph will be discreet and "divorce her quietly" (Mt 1:19). His inner strength does not come at the expense of the *seeming* weakness of Mary. His moral goodness is not a weapon for self-righteousness or condemnation. Joseph is a man who loves Mary. He does not stop loving her. They must now live apart but their love abides.

Have No Fear

Their human love is about to be elevated into the realm of the divine and play its crucial role in the birth of the Messiah. Joseph's dilemma concerning paternity, while protecting Mary, is resolved by the angel of the Lord in a dream. Mary can be taken as Joseph's wife. This child has been conceived by the Holy Spirit. This child will be called Jesus "because he will save his people from their sins" (Mt 1:21). Joseph does not have to be afraid. Love drives out all fear. The One who is love incarnate is about to come into the world.

How interesting that Matthew (and Luke as well) nowhere records any words of Joseph. He is a man of faith who speaks the language of direct, simple action. His is not a mindless, simplistic response, but an act of faith which will speak forever of what trust in God means. The evangelist tells us, "When Joseph awoke he did as the angel of the Lord had directed him and received her into his home as his wife" (Mt 1:24). There is about Joseph's action a similarity with the great Hebrew prophets. The Lord's word is accepted in trusting obedience because the One who calls is faithful and has been Emmanuel, "God is with us," from the beginning.

God Is For Us

Even though Mary and Joseph have received an angelic revelation that they are doing God's will, at a human level they must have wondered: *Where* is God in this situation? We believe God is with us but how?

The answer to these nagging questions is provided by the

angel in Joseph's dream: "She is to have a son and you are to name him Jesus because he will save his people from their sins" (Mt 1:21). With these words Joseph came to realize that God is not only *with* them; God is absolutely *for* them. In midst of sin, doubt, confession, and fear, God is both Emmanuel and Glorious Messiah, with us and for us. The Incarnation is God's total commitment in love to us. Everything human is taken into God through the Word made flesh. God is with us in the most profound, complete way. God becomes human in Jesus. Never again are we to doubt the divine commitment to humanity. Human dignity is forever confirmed.

Such a commitment by God to be with us does not come at a cheap price. The Incarnation cannot be separated from the Paschal Mystery. From the beginning Joseph knows that Jesus is the Savior. However, Jesus is not the political or military Messiah many had hoped for. Rather, Jesus is the Savior and Suffering Servant who will overcome sin and death (Is 53). God is *with* us in the flesh and *for* us as the Savior who will take away sins.

This profound connection between Incarnation and Paschal Mystery, crib and cross; the God who is at once with and for us, reveals divine love. Like Joseph, we may not always understand what God wants. At times we may not always experience his presence because of sin. Yet God is always Emmanuel. God in Jesus is always the Savior who takes away the sins of the world.

If only we would follow the example of Joseph, the quiet man of integrity, so God's messenger may speak in our dreams. When such occurs, may it be said of us that we "did as the angel of the Lord had directed" (Mt 1:24).

Prayer

O Lord, we often find ourselves in different situations, many of them of our own doing because we desire our will rather than yours.

We stray from your commands and turn away from your covenant.
We become lost and wonder if we shall ever find our way back to you.

During such times help us to remember that you are Emmanuel — God with us. Your only Son comes to us as one like us so that our poor humanity may be redeemed and restored to what you meant it to be from the beginning.

For Lord, you are not only with us; you are for us. Out of love you came in the flesh. Out of redeeming love you suffered and died for us so that sins would be forgiven. You offer us that lasting hope by conquering death and being our hope of glory.

Loving God, help us imitate Joseph. He is a man of quiet, strong faith. In the daily demands of our life, may we, too, walk by the insight of faith.
Help us to always know that you are near and never abandon us.
Regardless of the darkness, you shine with the Light of Truth and Life.
You are with us and for us. Let us journey toward you who are our lasting PEACE.

Reflection Questions

1. Do you find yourself benefitting from silent prayer and meditation? What form of prayer do you find deepens your relationship with Jesus? Do you find strength in reading and praying the Scriptures?
2. In what ways has God been with you during the past year? Do you sometimes feel that God is absent in your life? Why? What spiritual formation might help you grow closer to Jesus?
3. When you meditate on the crib and the cross of Jesus, what do these tell you about God's love? In what ways could you help others, especially these separated from the Church, to experience reconciliation during this Advent-Christmas season?

Saturday of Week Two
(Matthew 2:13-15)

The Dreamer

We Americans are a practical people. Short on theory; long on what works. We admire those who get things done. At some level we admire Martha in the Gospel of Luke. After all, she is busy about many things which allows Jesus and Mary to talk — and eat! A fundamental approach to problem solving is the pragmatic. We want to know what works. We are results oriented. We admire those who get the job done. This is not surprising since the practical and pragmatic were essential for survival in the New World. Food had to be obtained. Land had to be cleared and farmed. Security from hostile external forces had to be established. Action is required for all of these. There is little time to sit around and theorize or reach consensus. The race is to the swift acting and/or to those who boldly seize the occasion.

We like Joseph's quiet, strong manner. He is a man of moral strength. He is also an upright man who wants to protect the woman he loves. Joseph is also a practical man. He is a carpenter. He works with his hands and is skilled at what he does. Joseph must exercise good judgment if his work and creations are to be of value. In addition, possessing the practical skills of a carpenter, Joseph must also have something of the artist in him. Joseph not only fixes things; he also creates.

In addition to being a man of moral integrity, love, practical sense, and artistic creativity, Joseph is a dreamer. Better yet, he is a man to whom God communicates through dreams. Long before Freud, the Scriptures valued dreams as a profound way of understanding those truths which transcend the waking world. There is another level of consciousness that is set free with sleep. This highly symbolic world goes beyond the bounds of our rational, well-ordered, everyday lives. This is not to say that dreams are irrational. Rather, dreams are super-rational and lure us beyond the purely analytical and propositional. It seems as if we must be lured beyond the structures and meanings of everyday life if we are to hear the word of God. Our everyday expectations, especially those expectations structured by science and technology, leave little room for mystery and the symbolic.

During Joseph's time "the people were filled with anticipation" (Lk 3:15). The people were expecting the coming of the Messiah. Of course each person had his/her own belief about the Messiah. The symbolic, prophetic, and mysterious were part of the everyday world of Joseph and his times. Caution had to be exercised. It was an intense time. The zealot and fanatic were everywhere. Each claim to the Spirit and God's word had to be tested. By their fruits, you shall know them.

We turn to a series of Joseph's dreams in the Gospel of Matthew. They play an important role in our preparation for the birth of Jesus. The dreams of Joseph produce those fruits of the Spirit which help us to enter fully into the mystery of this season of God's Love.

An Unlikely Dreamer

Like the prophets and holy ones in the Hebrew Scriptures, Joseph is an unlikely candidate for his role in salvation history. There is no mention of Joseph possessing any mysterious powers, divine revelations concerning his birth, or angelic testimony about why Joseph was chosen in the first place. Joseph did not claim to be special or in possession of some extraordinary grace. He is not a professional religionist. His vocation is in the world. The fact that he is chosen from the world — much like the prophet Amos who was a shepherd and dresser of sycamores (Am 7:14) — only adds to his credibility. Joseph is not part of any school, cult, or religious group. Joseph is an upright man who makes his living as a carpenter and wants to have a family with Mary. Within these aspirations, God is at work.

The first dream of Joseph recorded by Matthew concerns his decision to divorce Mary quietly (Mt 1:19). The law is on his side. In fact, he could press the issue and make it public. But Joseph is a man pulled by his love for Mary and the requirements of the law. He will divorce her, but quietly. But there are no real winners in this situation. Sure, Mary will be spared public humiliation. However, the plans for their marriage and future happiness are gone. If only there was some way to resolve this conflict in a way that is honorable and preserves the prospects for future happiness.

The angel of the Lord comes to Joseph in a dream and tells of *God's* resolution to the situation. Joseph and Mary will be married, and it is the honorable thing. Even more, their marriage is part of the plan of salvation. For the child Mary is carrying is Jesus "who will save his people from their sins" (Mt 1:21). When their dilemma is taken up into God's plan, there is a resolution. Joseph and Mary had to be willing to go beyond the expected. They had to enter the realm of *faith*. Their leap of faith was not some irrational, desperate gamble. Rather, Joseph's dream was accepted with simple faith because the angel spoke on behalf of the One who is trustworthy. Mary accepted her annunciation, and Joseph followed his dream because they believed in the One who keeps promises.

The second dream of Joseph closely follows upon the first. Herod plans on killing Jesus. This is unknown to Joseph until the angel reveals it to him in a dream (Mt 2:13-15). The Holy Family must flee to Egypt and stay until the angel indicates it is safe to return to Nazareth. As in the first dream, Joseph's response reveals a man who trusts totally in the Lord: "Joseph got up and took the child and his mother and left that night for Egypt" (Mt 2:14).

Herod finally dies and the angel instructs Joseph to return

to Israel. However, the son of Herod, Archelaus, has assumed power. Like father, like son. The angel appears again to Joseph in a dream and tells him to settle in a town called Nazareth. The Holy Family once again follows the words of the Lord's angel. In so doing, they fulfill the prophecy: "Out of Egypt I have called my son" (Ho 11:1).

In this series of dreams after the birth of Jesus, we see God's providential care in response to worldly hostility. The birth of Jesus causes the forces opposed to the kingdom of God to even kill all "the boys two years old and under in Bethlehem and its environs" (Mt 2:16). However, God is the God of life and will not abandon those whom he has chosen. Salvation history has reached its definitive stage and will not be defeated by the forces of death.

Our Dreams

God's messenger and messages are not frozen in time or locked in some far-away place. God speaks to us today in the particular situation of our lives. The real questions are: Are we filled with expectations for the coming Messiah? Are we able to respond in simple faith to what the Lord is calling us to become? These are not academic questions but invitations to examine our lives in light of God's only Son — our Savior. Advent is that time of preparation when we sharpen our senses of sight and sound so as to be alert for God's appearance and word.

The dreams of Joseph tell us that no one who puts faith in God will ever be disappointed. God's promises are always kept; not as we expect but as God requires. God's promise to save is about to be realized. Do you not see it? Do you not hear its message? In the wonder of grace, look to the crib.

Prayer

O God, you come to us in waking days
and speak to us through our dreams
in the night.
Whether day or night, in light or darkness,
you come to us with the truth of
salvation. You come as one like us so
that our humanity can be elevated
to your original plan for our lives.
Such is our lasting peace.

Let your Holy Spirit touch our imagination
so that we may dream your dreams
and see your visions.
Help us to look
beyond the present to see
your past fidelity and our future hope
of eternal life.
But we are fearful.
We resist leaving the familiar.
We believe we know best.
We falter in faith.

Lord, you understand our weakness and
you give us your grace.
That is all we need
for the courage to hope;
the faith to surrender to your will;
and the love to respond to your LOVE.
As the days of Advent wind toward the
birth of the Messiah, let us dream.
Not some fantasy of our own creation
but the sure path to freedom, peace,
and salvation grounded in your faithful
promises.

Come, Lord Jesus!

Reflection Questions

1. In what ways have you experienced God calling you to accept some work on behalf of the Gospel? How did you discern this call? In what concrete ways did you respond to the call? What obstacles, if any, did you encounter?
2. Are you open to receive God's messengers? Do you find silent prayer a help in listening to God's word? Do you find yourself resistant to the idea of God speaking through others or events in life? Why?
3. How have you helped build the civilization of life and love? What are the ways the culture of death has influenced our public life? What can you do to help make public life more respectful of the human person?

Third Sunday of Advent
(Matthew 1:24)

Receptivity

The very idea of receptivity now carries a negative connotation. We often associate receptivity with passivity, laxity, and even a kind of indifference which borders on apathy. Ours is a culture which has come to value the proactive, aggressive, assertive, and self-promoting as essential to getting ahead. Receptivity carries with it a kind of laziness or sloth which ill serves those who want to get ahead in a highly competitive world. We value those who are up and doing and know what they want. After all, isn't the race to the swift, the prize to the strong, and the reward to those who are determined to have it all?

Yet, on closer inspection, might the bad press receptivity receives be ill deserved? Could there be some hidden virtue? The answer to both questions is yes. Authentic receptivity is at once a grace and a skill, a gift and a practice learned in countless ways over time. The receptive person is one who knows how to make welcome the guest, is open to what is new while respecting the past, and creative in responding to the unexpected. Receptivity is one of those virtues most needed for friendship and essential for marital love. The receptive person knows that sometimes in *receiving we give*; that is, we allow others to evidence their talents and share their gifts. It is a wisdom to let others be of service to us.

At this time of year, there is much flow between giving and receiving. Usually, we judge the occasion in terms of giving which often is measured materially. Yet, the lasting gift is the gift of self. The appropriate response is to know the value of such a gift and the grace to receive it with reverence. Too much of this season is about giving without receiving. Gifts become mere exchanges, a kind of balancing of the scales, often out of obligation to reciprocate. We feel after the exchange as empty as the box which once carried the gift. We don't know how to receive because the true meaning of giving is obscured beneath boxes, bows, ribbons, and a large credit-card bill for the new year.

The idea of receptivity is not often associated with Joseph. This is unfortunate as well as understandable given our culture. Yet on closer inspection, Joseph offers us much wisdom about the grace of receptivity as well as an invitation to enter deeply into the truth of the birth of the Messiah. To this grace and truth, we now turn our reflections.

Joseph's Receptivity

The Gospel of Matthew reveals the receptivity of Joseph in three ways: receptivity as *openness, creativity,* and welcoming *love.*

No doubt Joseph's life was well-ordered. He was a craftsman with standing in the community. He was about to marry the woman he loved. The future looked secure with job, home, wife, and family. There is much about this picture that is conventional and ordinary. In many ways Joseph's expectations would fit a familiar pattern shared by many men of his day.

In that ordinary, well-ordered world comes the shattering news that Mary is pregnant with a child not his own. Everything has changed. Promises are broken. Plans are canceled. What seemed so solid, melts into air. And of course, there is the question of what to do with Mary and the scandal. Joseph will divorce her quietly and try to move on with his life.

Yet, God has a different plan. Mary is pregnant through the power of the Holy Spirit. Joseph is to take her as his wife. The child to be born will be called Jesus because he is the Savior who will take away sins. All of this is part of God's plan for salvation. Joseph is being challenged to relinquish his *dreams* for God's *reality* — salvation. Joseph is being called to let go of his expectations so he can receive what the Lord will send. Joseph's receptivity to this new plan of God is expressed by his direct response of faith: "Joseph awoke and did as the angel of the Lord had directed him" (Mt 1:24).

In addition to receptivity as openness, Joseph also displays receptivity as a creative response to life. His plans for marriage seemed ended. By all rights of law and human emotion, he could have Mary exposed for what she appears to be. Yet, this is not the way Joseph responds. Rather than vengeance hiding behind legalism, Joseph will do the honorable thing but in a quiet way. Joseph receives a jolt to his plans, but he will not give in to meanness. Because he is receptive to what life sends his way, Joseph is able to creatively respond in such a way that both truth and love are joined. No, he is not the father; but, Mary will be shown compassion. This creative response bespeaks a man of maturity and creative receptivity.

Finally, Joseph's receptivity shows a hospitality toward the other. The Gospel of Matthew tells us that Joseph "received her into his home as his wife" (Mt 1:24). Genuine receptivity welcomes the other as other. There is a respect for the unique giftedness of others. Joseph receives Mary in all her uniqueness as his wife. This is not what he expected. It is important to note that Mary is *not taken* into his home nor *taken* as his wife. The evangelist carefully says that Joseph *received* Mary into his home as his wife. Mary and the child are gifts to Joseph. They are not property to be bought or prizes to be won. One can only *receive* such gifts in gratitude and loving respect.

Be Receptive

The life of Joseph teaches us a deep wisdom about the grace of receptivity. We are reminded that *all is gift*. As such, we are to live a life of receptivity and gratitude which allows us to give in an authentic way. We give out of love in response to having received love itself. There is no need to win approval, balance the scales of obligation, or impress in order to prove our worth. Such futile gestures only leave us empty.

Our lives take on true meaning when we are open to receive all God has to give. This will require a willingness to lay aside our well-developed plans so God can be present through us. Our creative receptivity will give us the eyes to see and the ears to hear the many ways the Holy Spirit is among and within us. And we will be able to receive the gift of the other as a gift from God. The other is not stranger, competitor, or enemy, but one like us.

It is only through Joseph- and Mary-like receptivity that we are able to see the One who is Other in the crib. In so doing we come to see that the Other One in the crib is God's unbounded love for us. The Other One in the crib is like us so that we may become reborn in his likeness.

Prayer

O God, we are so busy with all our many
projects and dreams.
We plan each day believing we know
what is best.
We resist surrender to your holy will
and your plan for our lives.
We find so many obstacles and reasons
for ignoring the many ways you
come to us.

Lord, quiet our hearts, still our fears,
and give peace to our spirits so
that we may center ourselves
in your will.
Give us that receptive heart we
find in Mary and Joseph.

Help us to live each day with a receptivity
that knows all life is a gift.
Gratitude fills us when we recognize
all that you give out of love.
In a special way we are grateful for
the gifts of others who enrich, challenge,
and strengthen our lives.

Above all, you give us your only Son for
our salvation.
During this Holy Season, let us be receptive
to the Child in the crib.
Let us see the One as the Other who saves;
the Other who redeems by
being one like us. Help us to become
more like him each day.

Reflection Questions

1. In what specific ways have you shown hospitality to others? How have you received the stranger in your church, community, school, or place of work? What keeps you from being open to the other? How can you overcome fear or lack of trust?
2. Do you experience life as gifts? In what concrete ways has God blessed you with the gifts of the Holy Spirit? In what ways have you shared God's gifts with others?
3. How have you been open to God's plans for the gift of life? In what ways has God surprised you with his gifts? How have you used these gifts? What has kept you from living a life of gratitude? How does prayer help open your heart to the gift of God who is Jesus?

Monday of Week Three
(Matthew 2:13-15)

Action

One of my father's favorite expressions is, "I can't hear a word you're saying, your actions speak too loud." Translation: actions drown out words. Stop saying one thing but doing something else. In the contemporary lingo — walk your talk.

Once upon a time, we expected our leaders to keep promises and match words with deeds. Unfortunately, we have now come to expect just the opposite. There is a cultural crisis of credibility when it comes to truth-telling. Cynically, we have come to believe that everything today is about "spinning a version" favorable to one's position or candidate. We answer Pilate's question, "What is truth?" by saying it is whatever story can be sold to the public. The role of "Spin Doctor" has now become an accepted part of the public landscape. What has resulted is a genuine disillusionment that causes apathy throughout society. When we see wrongdoing, we are told in the words of a song, "don't you believe your lying eyes." Even when we see something, don't rush to judgment before someone has a chance to interpret the act (put the proper spin on it). Image is everything and everything is open to interpretation.

Joseph seems strangely out of place in the culture of spin in the era of interpretation. He is not part of the well-connected or the religious elite. He is not found in the palaces of power. Joseph does not have an image problem because Joseph doesn't have an image! There is about Joseph a strength of character which is revealed in simple, direct action. He is uncomplicated yet deals with the complex; simple yet essential to God's love story of humankind; and straightforward in a world in which everyone has a line for every occasion. Joseph has no lines or gimmick. His is the eloquence of a life lived in the truth.

Integrity

Up until now, we have highlighted Joseph as the one who receives dreams and the one who is receptive to the surprising plan of God for salvation. These two qualities cannot be viewed in isolation from Joseph as a man of action. In effect, Joseph is an integrated man; that is, he receives messages in dreams and he *acts* on those dreams. Joseph avoids being an escapist who lives in some fantasy world. At the same time, Joseph is not a mindless actor with no sense of purpose or goal. Both dreams and action are present and integrated within Joseph.

This integration of dream and action means Joseph is a man of integrity (Mt 1:19). There is a sense of wholeness about him. Integrity translates to action. Simply put, Joseph is a man of truth. There is a oneness about what he receives in dreams and what he does. Lives are at stake. Joseph has a dream in which he is told to take Mary and Jesus to Egypt in order to escape the murderous plan of Herod. We are told, "Joseph got up and took the child and his mother and left that night for Egypt" (Mt 2:14). There is an immediacy of response, a decisiveness of plan, and a resolute will that bespeaks one who knows the seriousness of the moment. His quick action based on the dream proves successful. The Holy Family stays in Egypt "until the death of Herod" (Mt 2:15).

Faith As Action

The integration of dream and action reveals Joseph as a man of authentic faith. Often we fail to distinguish between faith and belief. A belief is a teaching we hold to be true. Beliefs tend to reside in the intellect and become part of a system as formal theology. Beliefs are expressed in propositions which can be evaluated as orthodox or heretical; a true belief as opposed to a false one.

Faith, though, is more genuinely expressed in the realm of action. Faith can be seen as the *active* expression of our beliefs. When we genuinely believe, we put that belief into practice. The practice of our beliefs, a living faith, is a sign that we have integrated the intellect with the will, knowledge with choosing, understanding with decision.

Joseph is a man in whom faith and belief are integrated. No doubt he was a man of God who firmly believed the promises of the Scriptures. He shared in the hopes for Israel and the promise of salvation. When the angel of the Lord speaks to him in a dream, Joseph acts without hesitation. His is not a mindless, robotic act, but rather one of faith-in-action based on the belief that God is to be trusted. For Joseph's belief in God is not an intellectual game but the deepest commitment of one's self to what is *really Real*. Throughout our encounter with Joseph, we see time and again a man of faith; a man in whom belief and faith, dream and action are integrated. Joseph does not blindly leap into action. Even less does he wager that by acting he has nothing to lose and everything to gain. Rather, Joseph's action expresses a total commitment to God's truthful word.

Belief and Faith Today

We face our own challenges concerning faith and belief in the contemporary culture of science and technology. For many God is dead, or absent, or there is an eclipse of God. We have the illusion that we are masters of our fate and the measure of all things. The works of our hands, and not those of God, become the ultimate source of meaning and truth.

Yet beneath the surface there is a disquiet, an anxiety, about the very things which reveal our power. We experience a crisis of belief in the dogma of scientific progress and doubts about faith in using technology to answer our deepest longings. The human spirit requires more than bread and machines. Our spirit yearns for that Spirit of truth which sets us free.

During this time of Advent, Joseph is a sure guide to the One who illuminates the mystery of existence. Joseph invites us to the crib where we find the One who is with us and for us. We see the God who never disappoints or abandons us. To see God in the crib requires a union of belief and faith. We are to believe in God who is totally committed to us. So deep is this loving commitment that God becomes one like us. To believe in such a God moves us to claim that faith which gives eternal life. We live in that faith which empowers us to act with love on behalf of the weak, poor, powerless, defenseless, and all who have no one to plead their case. We act in such a way because we believe that God acts in such a way toward us.

Into our fragmented world and anxious hearts, God acts with love. Joseph invites us to the crib. Can we believe such a God? Can we accept and act with such a love? Yes, Lord! Help our unbelief.

PRAYER

O Lord, help us to believe rightly so that
we might do your will in all things.
At times we become confused in thinking
about you. At times we fail to think
about you at all.
We are so involved with ourselves and
caught up in the things around us.
We claim you are silent, absent, or indifferent. Yet, it is really we who have
turned from you.

Bring us home to you. Let us follow the
example of your servant Joseph. You

speak to us in so many ways: friends,
family, events, and our innermost thoughts.
Yet again, we look away
and fail to see.

Yet, you never abandon us. Especially during
this Holy Season, you come in the most
profound expression of love for us — you
come as one like us.
All of this is too wonderful for us. Make
us humble so as to receive the Holy
Spirit of wisdom that draws us into
your mystery of love for us.

Like Joseph, let us put our belief into action.
Let our faith show your love each
day, especially to those most in need.
In loving, motivated by faith, we mirror
your love and goodness to us. Let us always
act with a belief in you and a faith
in the service of your love.

Reflection Questions

1. In what ways have you been able to integrate belief and faith? What have been the obstacles to such integration? In what ways does our society inhibit belief in God? What doubts do you wrestle with in your mind? How might they be resolved?
2. In what concrete ways has the example of Saint Joseph inspired you in this Advent season? How has your faith become stronger? In what specific ways have you put your faith into practice?
3. What does the Incarnation reveal about the nature of God? How has the Incarnation empowered you to be of greater service to others? What specific forms of service are you committed to in the coming New Year?

December 17th
(Matthew 2:19-23)

The Settler

The word "settler" unsettles us. For the word is filled with ambiguity. We attach both positive and negative meanings to the word.

American history glorifies the pioneer and pilgrim. We honor the adventurer who dares to go where no one has gone before. This bold breed takes risks and looks death in the face. The pioneer breaks new ground so that life will be better for those who come after them. The pilgrim leaves all that is sure and secure in order to find a better way to live. The pilgrim often sees his mission as part of God's plan, and he is under God's providence. The image of pilgrim is a prominent one in the Christian understanding of Church. We are a Pilgrim People; traveling by faith to our one true home which is heaven. Pilgrims are given special blessings and recognition as they travel to holy lands and sacred places. There are also times when pilgrimage takes on the urgency of a flight from danger. The Holy Family will come to know this well. The forces of death do not give up easily.

At the same time, we recognize the need for the settler and the settlement. At some point the pilgrimage must end, and the pilgrim reaches his destination. There is the adventure of discovery to be sure; likewise, there is the adventure of the daily grind which makes the new land a home. Without the settler, there are no roots. Families and communities cannot be formed without stability, order, infrastructure, and the development of civil society which protects basic rights. God's people must settle in the land he will give them. Their days of wandering in the desert must end. The very notion of being a people requires a homeland, a settlement which takes on a permanence for future generations. The nomadic life is too risky and must give way to those who dwell in the land.

Rather than seeing settler and pilgrim in conflict, it would be helpful to understand them in complementary terms. Certainly Joseph and the Holy Family did, for they were at various times in flight as well as settled. So far, we have reflected on Joseph and Mary in flight. They made their way to Bethlehem in obedience to Caesar Augustus' call for a census. Once Jesus is born, the Holy Family had to take flight into Egypt in order to avoid Herod's plan to kill Jesus. Once Herod died, the Holy Family was instructed to return to Nazareth. In these episodes of flight, we can see the courageous faith of Joseph. Less obvious is the faith that is needed once the Holy Family settles in Nazareth. It is to that faith and life we now turn our reflections.

Another Dream

The journey homeward involves a dream. The Holy Family has been in exile in Egypt. The Lord's angel warned Joseph of Herod's design on Jesus' life. This exile in Egypt and return to Israel is deeply theological and is at the center of Israel's identity as a people. The Holy Family's exile in Egypt represents Israel's bondage during the time of Moses. As Israel was in slavery so the Holy Family is in bondage due to the murderous intent of Herod. As Israel had suffered under Pharaoh, so the Holy Family suffers under Herod. It is only upon leaving Egypt that the Hebrews became a people in the land God provides. The Holy Family represents the New Israel from whom the Messiah will set captives free from sin and death.

The Gospel of Matthew's purpose is to show that Jesus is the Messiah. He is the Promised One who will liberate his people. However, this liberation will be more profound than in the days of Moses and the Exodus. The return from Egypt is a sign of hearts turning to God and the establishment of the new People of God.

The Homecoming

The days of wandering are about to end. The adventure of faith will enter a new, more hidden, but no less important phase. The Holy Family will return from their flight into Egypt in order to settle in Nazareth. Like Israel, the Holy Family experiences its own time of bondage, exodus, wandering, and final settlement in a place the Lord provides. They are called out of Egypt by the Lord's angel and told to return to Israel. However, such a return will not be easy. For Herod's successor, Archelaus, son of Herod the Great and brother of Herod Antipas, is just as ruthless. Hence, the Holy Family must settle in Nazareth. But this too is part of God's plan and carries theological significance.

The prophet (probably Isaiah in 11:1) speaks of the Messiah as a "sprout" or "shoot." Even though the dynasty of David can be cut down or experience hardships, God will never forget his promises. The Davidic line will be re-established and the Messiah spring forth. God will plant the Holy Family in Nazareth and the Messiah "shall be called a Nazarene" (Mt 2:23). Even when the forces of darkness seem most powerful and victorious, God acts so as to ensure salvation history. God's kingdom will be established and the forces opposed to God's reign will be defeated.

Settled In a Town

The Holy Family finally arrives to settle "in a town called Nazareth" (Mt 2:23). The angels no longer appear. The wise men have returned to their own country. Herod is dead and Archelaus is far away. The Holy Family will slip into the normal patterns of Nazarene life. God's ways and the adventure of faith must be uncovered in the everyday demands of life. It should never be forgotten that the Holy Family is a *human* family with all the needs and pressures that faced any family of the time. Jesus will grow up in the house of his carpenter father and loving mother. They will provide Jesus with all the human things he needs: the basic physical necessities in addition to the religious training of the day. Jesus is the Son of God and also the son of Joseph and Mary. The human formation of his character and personality are entrusted to Joseph and Mary.

Years after their initial arrival in Nazareth, when Jesus is twelve, he goes with his parents to the Passover in Jerusalem. Jesus gets separated from them. They find him in the Temple with the religious intellectuals of the day. Jesus was a gifted child. "All who heard him were amazed at his intelligence and his answers" (Lk 2:47). After they scold him for causing them to worry, we are told that Jesus returned to Nazareth with Joseph and Mary. While being under their authority, Jesus "progressed steadily in wisdom and age and grace before God and men" (Lk 2:52). This evaluation tells us that Joseph and Mary were good parents to a gifted child. Jesus, while gifted, does progress through the normal human stages of development experienced by any young person of the time.

The settled context of the home, with Joseph and Mary, is the foundational place for Jesus. The Messiah is also a human boy in need of formation and maturity. Jesus will develop his humanity under their loving care, less dramatic than previous episodes, hidden away from the writings of the evangelists. This quiet phase of faith, however, is essential for the man who will emerge from the desert and proclaim his theme: "Reform your lives! The kingdom of heaven is at hand" (Mt 4:17). It is the same man who will open his arms on the cross and proclaim, "Now it is finished" (Jn 19:30). In the formative years with Joseph and Mary, the man was developing inside the boy. The settled home of Nazareth helped form the Messiah whose birth, death, and resurrection is our hope of an everlasting home in God.

Prayer

O Lord, your Holy Spirit calls us each day to
greater lives of love and service. You call us
to live the great adventure of faith
in new and creative ways.
Yet, we are fearful and want to remain
in our comfortable everyday world.
We want security.
We believe this is peace.
This is not your peace.

Liberate our hearts with grace
so that we may accept
an invitation to the Kingdom.
Let us learn from Joseph
that you never invite us
to any place
that your love has not prepared for us.
We can go in new places
because your love is always present
to and for us.

Lord, we also need to show faith and love
in the daily routines of our lives.
Help us to see and know you
in our homes, schools,
places of work, and play,
and in all the daily ways
that we influence others.
Let us see in the ordinary
your extraordinary love.
Let us experience your presence in a world
that can be cold and indifferent.
Let us speak your truth in love to a
world which lives with illusions and idols.

God, in our high adventures and everyday
routine, we belong to you. Throughout
we need your grace so that we might walk
by faith and live through love.
In so doing we shall be a people of hope.
A hope that one day we shall be home with you.

Reflection Questions

1. In what specific ways have you been a pioneer for your faith? How did God's grace help in these situations? What was the reaction of other people?
2. In what specific ways have you experienced God's grace in the ordinary, everyday activities of daily life? How has God's grace helped redeem the most mundane of responsibilities? How does God's grace help you creatively meet the ordinary demands of home, school, or work?
3. How has your family life found inspiration from the Holy Family? What did you learn from the example of Joseph, Mary, and Jesus when you faced challenging situations? The routines of everyday family life?

December 18th
(Luke 2:41-52)

The Background

As we bring our reflections about Joseph to a close, it seems fitting that he recedes to the background. Is this consignment to a position not on center stage a sign of disrespect or an evaluation of his part in salvation history? The answer is a resounding "no" to both questions. Saint Joseph is held in the highest esteem by the Church as the patron of workers as well as the model for fatherhood. His part in the birth of the Messiah is greatly honored in the Gospel of Matthew. Joseph is the man of dreams and action whose decisive response to the angel is crucial for Mary and Jesus.

The movement of Joseph to the background is highly theological and profoundly spiritual. It not only tells us something about the man Joseph, but it also reveals a deep insight into God the Father, and the nature of fatherhood itself.

Measure of the Man

When it came time for John the Baptist to grow less so Jesus could be more, he rejoiced to see that time of fulfillment (Jn 3:30). It is much the same with Joseph. His movement to the background is done out of recognition that Jesus is the center of salvation, and Mary will go on to play a key role in their son's future. Joseph did all things well and is able to relinquish his influence to others. However, the fact that Joseph becomes silent and moves to the background does not mean his influence is obliterated. Jesus will always carry the influence of his earthly father. When the voice from heaven declares on the banks of the Jordan at

Jesus' baptism, "This is my beloved Son. My favor rests on him" (Mt 3:17), this is also a commentary about Joseph. For the beloved Son of the heavenly Father was entrusted to an earthly father — Joseph. The favor or grace that rests on Jesus is an acknowledgment that Joseph is also loved and favored by God. For Joseph has been worthy of the trust to be father of Jesus.

Joseph in the background is in reality more influential, not less. Coaches know true development of talent and the refinement of skills takes place outside of practice by the extra work of dedicated players. Teachers know their influence is often after school and outside the formal setting of a class period and specific subject. Good parents know their influence is often indirect and secondary. It is around the table and in casual discussions that parental influence is greatest. Joseph does not need the spotlight to help form Jesus or show his authority. No doubt much of Joseph's influence on Jesus took place through working in the carpenter shop. We do not take the measure of Joseph by the volume of words spoken or the number of episodes recorded. The measure of Joseph as a man, husband, and father is found in Luke's Gospel: "Jesus, for his part, progressed steadily in wisdom and age and grace before God and men" (Lk 2:52).

God The Father

The fatherhood of Yahweh is unlike any other god or deity. Some of the neighbors of Israel understood their chief god as the father of the other gods or cosmic forces. The fatherhood of Yahweh is understood in two ways. Through Yahweh's creative word, everything comes into existence; and, secondly, Yahweh's authority is expressed through faithful love for all creation, especially the poor. Yahweh is no indifferent or absent God but is intimately involved with his creation. Even when things go awry, Yahweh remains faithful and promises to send the Savior.

In the fullness of time, God's fatherly authority and love

becomes visible in the Incarnation. The creative Word and Wisdom of God becomes flesh (Jn 1:14). Yahweh is the ultimate promise keeper whose love is creative and salvific. From the time of the Fall (Gn 3), through the prophets, and now to a small town called Bethlehem, God's promise of the Messiah is about to be fulfilled. Heaven itself cannot contain its joy at the birth of the One who is Peace. The heavenly host burst forth in praise of God: "Glory to God in the high heaven, peace on earth to those on whom his favor rests" (Lk 2:14).

The Fatherhood of Joseph

Yahweh's authority over creation and his people Israel is expressed through love, discipline, compassion, formation, and a deep commitment to the poor. We see all of these at work in the fatherhood of Joseph. For his authority is one of protection and guidance. In the most difficult of circumstances, Joseph accepts each challenge and instruction as a way of drawing deeper into love. Joseph is disciplined so he can be decisive in moving his family to safety when the need arises. Joseph shows compassion toward Mary in not wanting to expose her to the law. He is a father of simple, steadfast love who acts on God's word and provides for his family in all things. The authority of Joseph is a moral foundation in that truth expressing itself in faithful love.

The fatherhood of Joseph is also wise and humble, for Joseph knows that all human authority is limited and even the deepest of human bonds are provisional. Joseph, like Mary, will need to let Jesus go. There is a deeper mission and higher purpose for this one born wonderfully in time and space. Jesus' time with Joseph and Mary is short. The message of the Kingdom will take him beyond Nazareth and his father's carpenter shop. Joseph and Mary must love enough to let go.

We see a glimpse of this with the finding of Jesus in the Temple (Lk 2:41-50). The parents are both astonished and also upset that something might have happened to their son. Jesus' reply is an indication of what is to come: "'Why did you search for me? Did you not know I had to be in my Father's house?' But they did not grasp what he said to them" (Lk 2:48-50). There will come a time when Joseph's house will be but a memory. From that earthly home much will abide. Yet Jesus' heavenly Father must be revealed; the Kingdom proclaimed; and the time of deliverance made public to the world.

Luke goes on to tell us that Mary "kept all these things in memory" (Lk 2:51). We are not told about Joseph's reaction. Was it one of pride in a son who is so brilliant? Pride in a son growing in independence? Perhaps. There may also be the bittersweet recognition that love respects freedom and the willingness to share with a larger world a sign of that love-in-freedom. The temptation to hold on must have been great for Joseph. Here is his only son talking about his Father's house in a mysterious way. Yet Joseph no doubt sensed that this was another part of God's plan for salvation. This was another call to let the Father's will be done on earth as it is in heaven. The earthly father Joseph would obey once again.

Luke tells us that Joseph and Mary didn't understand what Jesus meant. Not surprising. So much of parenting is mysterious. Parents walk by faith. Only in retrospect do we see the meaning and truth of things. In the present we often see as in a glass, darkly (1 Cor 13:12). We must trust in the Divine Providence which orders all things to the good. Joseph so trusted throughout his life. The letting go of Jesus to be in his Father's house is just one more loving surrender to the God who is faithful.

Prayer

O God, who is our loving Father,
who speaks all things into existence.
Your mighty word gives life
to all living creatures.
Your life-breath fills us with life.
We are wonderfully made
in your image and likeness.

Help us each day to be
about your business of salvation.
Guide us in your truth
so that we may live
and proclaim the Gospel.
Let us be found in your house
doing your will.
For all of creation
is your earthly dwelling.
There is no place for us to hide.
There is no corner of creation
that escapes your loving providence.

Lord, your love is shown
in the gift of earthly parents.
Let parents mirror
your authority and love for their children.
Help each family to be like the Holy Family.
Let each family be rooted
in your truth and trusting of your
providential care.

Let the spirit of Joseph be with parents
as they love their children in freedom;
a freedom which directs their lives
to your truth and peace.

Reflection Questions

1. In what ways has your family been a blessing to you? A challenge? What guidance can the Holy Family offer in facing the challenges of family life in today's world?
2. In what specific ways have you been called to do God's will while serving in the background? Do you feel the need to be the center of things? Why? In what creative ways might God be calling you to serve by recognizing the gifts of others?
3. How has God challenged you to relinquish some project or relationship for a greater purpose? Were you resistant to letting go? Why? Were you able to finally see some deeper meaning to your surrender?

MARY

As the days of Advent wind down to a precious few, the cry of "Maranatha" beats stronger in our hearts. And what more fitting way to end our season of anticipation than with Mary. For through her faith, her "yes" of faith, God takes on a human face in Jesus. On behalf of all of us, Mary spoke. Her receptivity to the Word was not only for herself but for all humankind. Mary is the New Eve in whom, and through whom, the Messiah will be born. She is the Mother of God and the Mother of us all. For in her the divine and the human become one in Jesus, the Word made flesh.

It is quite natural to get caught up in high moments of Mary's life along with the honorific titles bestowed on her by the Church. All of this is important as we contemplate the role of Mary in salvation history. At the same time we should never forget that Mary is the *human* daughter of Joachim and Ann. Jesus is "born of a *woman* under the law" according to the Scriptures. Such bluntness is not meant to demean Mary but to exalt God's grace building on the human. Mary's humanity is just as essential as the humanity of Jesus for God's plan of salvation. Just like with Joseph, God does not negate the humanity of Mary but reveals what he intended from the beginning of creation.

Throughout our reflections about Mary as a figure around the crib, we will consider "the great things" the Almighty has done for her and by extension for each of us. The significant episodes in Mary's life must always be understood in terms of what they reveal about Christ and what they reveal for the Church. Mary's life is filled with Christological, ecclesiastical, and anthropological truth. Mary is one with Christ, the Church, and our shared humanity. Mary is never just for herself, by herself. Rather, Mary is thoroughly *communio*, that is, a person with, for and within the community we call Church and the community of persons we call the Trinity. In looking to Mary, we see what it means to be a true disciple. Mary also reveals the true mission and message of the Church: bring forth the Word made flesh.

Such an understanding of Mary is laid with centuries of reflection and prayer. Yet we must never lose sight of the origins of our encounter with Mary. The witness of Scripture remains normative for our understanding of Mary and her truth for our lives. It is in Nazareth that we first meet "a virgin betrothed to a man named Joseph of the house of David" (Lk 1:27). We are told the virgin's name was "Mary" (Lk 1:27). She will be visited by the angel Gabriel with the most dramatic news to ever be received in the world. The Messiah is coming, and Mary is going to play an essential role. The time longed for by all the prophets is about to be fulfilled. The mighty work of salvation is about to enter human history.

Our hearts skip a beat; we lean forward; and we take a breath in anticipation. Mary reaches out to us with the invitation to come around the crib. Come and see what God's love has done for you.

We dare to draw near.

December 19th
(Luke 1:26-38)

Annunciation

Each day we are inundated with messages. From e-mail to the junk-mail which comes the old fashion way; our daily life is one of being informed, put on notice, or just plain talked at! As a defense mechanism, we have developed a screening process or filter. We learn to selectively listen in order to avoid sensory and info overload. The danger is we can miss a significant announcement when it comes our way. There is just so much to process. The superficial drives out the substantive.

The definitive phase of salvation history is about to commence. God will no longer speak through the prophets. God's messengers, angels, are making their final contacts before the birth of the Messiah. God is gong to speak directly through the Word who will become flesh. God is going to enter human history and the human condition. But the entrance must at once be clearly from God's side, all the while involving the totality of what is human. The initiative will be from God. The response to the divine overture must come freely from the human side. This response will come from one selected by God's mysterious plan. The one selected will be "full of grace," that is free from sin; so, the Word will be conceived by the Spirit in holiness.

God is about to speak. The message will be heard. Yet the drama is only beginning to unfold.

The One Chosen

In the Gospel of Matthew, Joseph is the central figure leading up to the birth of Jesus and the important events that immediately follow (the flight into Egypt and the subsequent return to settle in Nazareth). With the Gospel of Luke, Mary occupies center stage in the drama of salvation history. For it is she to whom the angel appears and announces her selection as mother of the Savior. Mary is active in visiting Elizabeth and responds to her greeting with a beautiful canticle. Mary is the central figure in the birth of Jesus and treasures all these things in her heart. Subsequent events have Mary playing the lead role as with the finding of Jesus in the Temple. It is Mary who speaks to Jesus about their anxiety over his being separated from them. Clearly from the perspective of Luke and the needs of his audience, Mary is the highly favored, chosen one. God's plan is not limited to a select few nor confined by human expectations. God's message of salvation is for everyone. God continues to surprise as he selects the unexpected (a virgin, women, the poor, and sinners) to accomplish his purpose. No one is outside the touch of God's grace. The Good News about to be proclaimed and made visible is for all the peoples of the earth (Lk 24:46-49).

We are never explicitly told, as with Joseph, why Mary was chosen to be the mother of the Messiah. Similar to Matthew's introduction of Joseph as a man of integrity, Luke introduces Mary as "a virgin betrothed to a man named Joseph, of the house of David" (Lk 12:27). As Luke proceeds, we are told Mary is "highly favored" and comes to understand herself as "the servant of the Lord" (Lk 1:38). No doubt, there were many other virgins who found favor with God and did their best to be his servant. Again, we must ask: Why Mary?

The answer lies in the mysterious plan of salvation formed by God from all eternity. Mary was pre-destined yet *totally free* to give her consent to be the mother of the Messiah. In the words of the Second Vatican Council:

> The Father of mercies willed that the Incarnation should be preceded by assent on the part of the predestined mother, so that just as a woman had a share

in the coming of death, so also should a woman contribute to the coming of life.

Mary is the New Eve, through whom God will restore humanity to its original intended holiness. Mary, freed from all sin by her Immaculate Conception, as a foresign of the work of the Messiah, is completely open to receive the Word of Life that will become flesh in her.

Deeply Troubled

In the midst of her being declared highly favored and called to rejoice, we see a very human Mary responding in a very natural way: "She was deeply troubled by his words and wondered what his greeting meant" (Lk 1:29). It is an awesome thing to be addressed by God, especially since Mary is being chosen as the Mother of the Messiah. Not only the substance of the angel's message but the very process fills her with wonderment. Mary is a virgin who will be with child!

Joseph faced the situation of being betrothed to Mary who was with a child not of his making. Mary will become pregnant with *the* child conceived out of the normal course of things. To both Joseph and Mary, the words of the angel are the same: "Do not fear" (Lk 1:30). Fear is natural. God's grace is supernatural and builds on human nature so that the divine will can be realized. It is faith motivated by love that drives out all fears (1 Jn 4:18). The removal of fear by grace empowers Joseph to take Mary as his wife. That same grace, overcoming fear, liberates Mary to say, "I am the servant of the Lord. Let it be done to me as you say" (Lk 1:38).

The call of God is always about service. There is no hint of arrogance or pride on Mary's part at being chosen as the Mother of the Messiah. Mary presents herself as unworthy of the role she is about to assume. This humility of spirit and obedience to God's will contrast with the first Eve. In the garden Eve was overcome with pride and rebellion. Her reach exceeded her grasp. She drew Adam into the Fall as they rejected being creatures in the desire to be the creators. The result was sin, alienation, banishment, and death (Gn 3:23-24). By contrast, Mary is the humble, lowly servant of the Lord.

Through the receptive surrender to the angel's message and the Word becoming flesh in her, a new humanity will be born. She will be mother to the new creation established by Jesus, the new Adam. (Rm 5:12-21). In place of sin, she will be the one full of grace; alienation will be overcome by love; banishment will give way to homecoming; and the reign of death will be ended by the One who is Light and Life.

The exalted position of Mary does not place her above humanity or withdraw her from the needs of others. Mary is the woman for others as her son will be the man for others. The other in this case is Mary's kinswoman, Elizabeth, who "has conceived a son in her old age" (Lk 1:36).

With Mary, the Annunciation leads directly to the Visitation.

Prayer

O Lord, each day you come to us with your
grace. Each day is a gift for us to
use in knowing you more deeply and sharing
your love with others.

We need to be like Mary: a receptive
servant of your Word. Too often we
are filled with pride. We desire our own
way rather than yours.
Pride and rebellion keep us from
humbly acknowledging your greatness.

We often grasp for the passing rewards
of this world rather than setting
our hearts on you. We seek the praise
of human beings rather than the glory
of your unfailing love.

Fear is too often with us, not the fear of your
presence but the fear that comes from
setting our hearts on that which passes away.
Let us each be mindful that with you
is fullness of life forever.

O God, you looked on Mary your servant.
Look on us as well. Let us in our
confusion be reassured by your truth.
When we are lost, let us know that
you are always present.
When we want to do our will, let us
be the servant and handmaid of your Word.

Let us know your peace which is beyond all
understanding. Let us be instruments of
your peace each day. For lasting peace is from you.

Reflection Questions

1. During the season of Advent, how has God's living word come to you? What has God asked of you? How have you responded? Generously? With fear? Rebellion?
2. In what specific ways have you been a servant of the Lord's word? Do you meditate daily on the Scriptures? Do you find that reading the Bible is a source of strength and guidance? How?
3. Have you been deeply troubled in recent times in your spiritual life? Why? Has prayer been a source of comfort and discernment? Do you believe God is asking of you more than you can possibly do? Where is God's grace during these times?

December 20th
(Luke 1:39-45)

The Visitation

Pope John Paul II has written and preached that the true meaning of discipleship is revealed through what he calls, "the Law of the Gift." By this the pope means that the decision to follow Jesus is at once the decision to deny oneself, die to oneself, and to transcend oneself by loving God and donating oneself to others. The Law of the Gift is the complete abandonment of oneself to God in response to the ultimate Gift of God — Jesus Christ. True disciples of Jesus give themselves completely to the Word made flesh. At the heart of the Christian life and the deepest meaning of this season, is the God who holds nothing back at Bethlehem and gives everything at Golgotha. Discipleship is the individual's response to Jesus' emptying and surrender, to and for us, so that we might be born anew.

The Law of the Gift is at the heart of the Gospel and stands in contrast to the Law of Self-Promotion. From the beginning, there has been in the human heart the desire to love the self to the exclusion of everyone and everything else. The self grasped at divinity in hopes of becoming like God and replacing God. Pride and self-will drive us to be the center of the universe. Everyone and everything becomes a means to *our* ends or desires. To give the self is to die — without hope of resurrection. There is no transcendence — only my desires which are supreme. Earthly life becomes the Golden Calf which leads to death. We are driven to promote the self against the dying of the light.

These two laws are in conflict within the human heart and all of history as well. Gift or Imperial Self are the two roads which are open before us as we make our earthly pilgrimage. Which is the road traveled that leads to life in abundance? Which path is the one, wide and inviting, that leads to death? We look to Mary as that sure guide on the road less traveled which brings us to the crib. For it is at the crib that the Law of the Gift becomes visible. God speaks the Only Son into the world and our very being. We can dare follow the Law of the Gift because the One who is gift has shown us the way. He says, "Be not afraid!"

Set Out In Haste

Mary is the embodiment of the Law of the Gift. Who could blame Mary if she began to bask in the afterglow of her annunciation? She had just been told she would be the mother of the Savior. With this greatest of privileges comes the expected perks of human respect, deference for one in her exalted position, and a general catering to by others befitting the Mother of God. Clearly this would be an opportunity for Mary to be served. Not only is she with child, but the child she carries is the Son of God.

Yet such is not the case with Mary. Her annunciation is a cause for Mary to be deeply troubled (Lk 1:29). Even after the angel explains the plan of God, there is no mention of Mary's understanding what will take place. Mary as "servant of the Lord" totally surrenders to the will of God. There is about Mary a complete openness and trust that God's will is the best. Rather than claiming a special status, Mary's response is one of accepting in total trust "the greatness of the Lord" (Lk 1:46).

There is within Mary's annunciation a second declaration as well by the angel. "Know that Elizabeth your kinswoman has conceived a son in her old age; she who was thought to be sterile is now in her sixth month, for nothing is impossible with God" (Lk 1:36-37). The Law of the Gift and the Gospel of Life are bursting forth in these days of God's unbounded grace. In place of sterility, there is life; in place of barrenness, the Lord's grace is at work; and Elizabeth's reproach gives way to a celebration of God's grace. Elizabeth will also be directly blessed by God's gift of life. Her son will herald the Messiah.

Of course, the annunciation of Mary is the greater. She will become pregnant through the power of the Holy Spirit. Mary will be the Mother of the Savior. We might expect that it would be proper for Elizabeth to come to Mary. The Law of the Gift confounds the etiquette of this world. It is *because* Mary has been so blessed by God's Gift that she sets out, "proceeding in haste into the hill country to a town of Judah, where she entered Zechariah's home and greeted Elizabeth" (Lk 1:39-40). Mary is the model of Christian discipleship. She goes in haste to be with Elizabeth in *her* joy. She goes to be with Elizabeth in order to share her needs. Not only is Mary the servant of the Lord, Mary is also the woman for others. God's gift of the Savior does not cause Mary to turn inward or become self-absorbed. Just the opposite. Mary, in haste, goes to be with and for Elizabeth.

The Baby Leapt for Joy

With the visitation, Mary provides us with the essential mission of the Church and for the individual Christian — bring Jesus to others. The very presence of Jesus causes John to "leap for joy." The good news of salvation brings joy to all the world. It is a joy, a gift of the Holy Spirit, that comes with the experience of Jesus and the Gospel. The long reign of sin and death will not last forever. God's reign will remove the ultimate power of sin and the lasting sting of death. The human moment of two mothers coming together also bespeaks the in-breaking of the divine. Grace builds on nature to reveal the saving power of God. One who was barren, one who is a virgin; both will bring forth new life. One child will grow to be the voice crying in the wilderness. The other child will be the One who both preaches the Kingdom and *is* the Kingdom. All of creation cannot help but break forth in joy with the heavenly host, "Glory to God in high heaven, peace on earth to those on whom his favor rests" (Lk 2:14).

The Law of the Gift fills us with joy. Advent is our time of preparation for the visitation. We are close to the Gift beyond price. About to be born to us is *the* Savior. Are we able to feel the joy and liberation of the fruit of Mary's womb? Are we able to be Holy Spirit-filled so that we too can receive Mary into our hearts? Can we too be one with Elizabeth in proclaiming, "Blest are you among women and blest is the fruit of your womb"? Can our hearts also leap with joy in anticipation of Jesus? We can say our "yes" to each of these if Elizabeth's words to Mary can be said of us: "Blest are those who *trust* that God's words will be fulfilled."

We can have such a trust by letting the words of the angel to the shepherds be ours: "You have nothing to fear! I come to proclaim good news to you" (Lk 2:10).

Prayer

O God, let us to be open to your Word
in imitation of Mary.
Yes, we have our fears.
Yes, we are so self-absorbed
in ourselves and the work of our hands.
We are too indifferent to the needs
of those around us.
You alone can liberate us
from our isolation.

Your Gift of the Son shows us that
the essence of life is found in
self-giving, self-surrender, and
self-denial which brings us
through the crib, cross, and empty
tomb. Which brings us to
that love which gives eternal life.

We are afraid of giving ourselves. We
may be rejected, found inadequate,
or we fear that in giving ourselves we

will be lost.
Yet Mary's reception of you as Gift
empowers her to give as well.
In giving as we have been given,
the Law of the Gift comes full circle.
The Law of the Gift breaks our fear
and liberates us to go out of ourselves.

Lord, send your Holy Spirit of joy into
our hearts. Let our hearts burn with love
and leap for joy in your presence.
Let us bring you, the Good News, to all
whom we meet. Let us be instruments
of your gift of love without end. Amen.

Reflection Questions

1. In what specific ways have you experienced God's Law of the Gift? How did you respond to such experiences? Did these experiences empower you to be a gift to others? How?
2. How have you struggled with the Law of the Gift? In what ways have you given in to the Law of Self-Promotion? Have you taken specific steps to overcome your pride? What are they? Have these steps been helpful?
3. How have God's gifts of grace empowered you to help others? Have you been a gift to the sick, lonely, and shut-ins? How have these visits to the forgotten been a gift to you?

December 21st
(Luke 1:46-56)

Canticle

Theme songs are part of American pop culture and play an important role in many relationships. During the forties and the era of the Big Bands of World War II, each band had a theme song along with a particular singer or group. When you heard "Moonlight Serenade," the band had to be Glenn Miller. Bob Eberly and Helen O'Connell sang about those "Green Eyes" and a girl named "Tangerine." More recently, Frank Sinatra's signature song was "My Way." The Beatles sang to every swooning girl, "I Want to Hold Your Hand." The list goes on and on.

Many married couples can trace their first date, dance, or proposal to the song that was playing and became "our song." Each time the music is played or sung, the chords of memory are strummed as well. We return to that special moment or occasion that changed our lives. We become one with the initial experience, and we experience the same emotions all over again as if for the very first time. Such is the power of music and memory.

The Bible is filled with theme songs called canticles. These hymns of praise are sprinkled throughout the Scriptures. The canticles are often centered around the theme of promise/fulfillment and are most appropriate for the infancy narrative. The Gospel of Luke contains four canticles; three of which are attributed to human beings and one to the heavenly host. The human canticles found in Luke are the Magnificat (1:46-55), the Benedictus (Zechariah's Canticle, 1:67-78), and the Nunc Dimittis (Simeon's hymn of praise at Jesus' presentation in the Temple, 2:28-32). The fourth hymn is the Gloria in Excelsis Deo sung by the angels in praise of God at the birth of Jesus (2:13-14).

Biblical canticles serve as hymns of praise to God for his fidelity to the covenant. Yahweh is a promise keeper. Because the Lord has been faithful in the past, there is every reason to trust that God will be faithful in the future. Yahweh does not go back on his word or abandon his people. Canticles acknowledge the mighty works of God in the here and now. Such recognition evokes the deepest expression of prayer — the praise of God. It is to Mary's canticle, her Magnificat, that we now turn, for her theme song captures the most profound truths about God and the child in the crib.

The Magnificat

Mary is the first disciple of the Kingdom of God. Her canticle opens with her "whole being" directed to the "greatness of the Lord." Mary is filled with joy that comes to those for whom God is Savior. Mary has received the gift of life. In her dwells the One who is son of David and Son of God (Lk 1:31-33). Mary experiences first-hand the Law of the Gift. God empties himself into the human condition and in humility accepts the cross for our salvation (see the great Pauline hymn in Philippians 2:6-11). From this gift of God's only Son as Savior, joined with Mary's acceptance of the Word, the new age of grace is about to dawn. All of this is the work of the Lord.

The opening verse of the Magnificat places Mary within the Old Testament tradition of great women within God's plan of salvation. The mother of Samuel, Hannah, is presented as a handmaid of the Lord. She sings a hymn of praise to the Lord for not forgetting her and blessing her with a son (1 S 1:11; 2:1-10). Likewise, there is a connection with Judith who is "blessed among women" (Jdt 13:18; 16:11). Mary is at once a continuation of the Hannah-Judith motif as well as its perfection, for Mary is blessed among women in a way like no other. Mary is mother to the Savior.

Like Hannah and Judith, Mary never forgets that she is the

recipient of God's gift. Mary, like her two sisters in faith, understands herself as representative of the *anawim*. Literally, the term means the "poor ones," that is the materially poor as well as those who must rely completely on God.

The *anawim* are the weak, the poor, the powerless, those who live on the margin of society. They are the invisible ones who are ignored by the community as being of no account. Yet they are precious to the Lord. The *anawim* place their trust completely in God who never abandons those who cry out to him. Mary never loses sight that she has been favored by the Lord in his mercy and not because of her merits. Furthermore, Mary associates with the "poor ones" of Yahweh who totally trust that God's promises will be kept. The good news of salvation, first revealed to her, is now associated with the *anawim*: the lowly are raised to high places; the hungry are satisfied; the lowly are exalted; and mercy is extended to those who live in awe of God. The mighty, that is, the self-sufficient and arrogant, are humbled; the poverty of the rich is exposed; and the smug are filled with anxiety. In the Magnificat of Mary, we hear the echo of the Beatitudes that Jesus will preach in Luke's Gospel (Lk 1:46-55; 6:20-26). God's decisive action is taking place in that "the poor have the gospel preached to them; liberty is proclaimed to captives; release to prisoners; and the blind see" (Lk 4:18-19). Salvation is at hand!

Greatness of the Lord

Praise is not flattery. Praise is always grounded in the truth about God and the reasons for acknowledging the Lord's greatness. Mary's Magnificat is centered in what the *Lord* has done for her as pure gift. Her recognition of the gift fills Mary with joy and moves her to proclaim the greatness of the Lord: Yahweh has kept the covenant; he has chosen one who is lowly (a poor one); Mary will not only be called great by all women but by all *gen-*

erations. In the Bible, Leah is called fortunate by all women; Elizabeth calls Mary blessed among women; and clearly Mary is greater than them all, for her blessedness extends throughout history (Gn 30:13; Lk 1:42). Even in her fear at the words of the angel, Mary is told not to be afraid but know that God's holy mercy (*hesed*) is "from age to age" (Lk 1:50).

With the end of verse 50 of the Magnificat, we make a transition in recounting the greatness of the Lord. The mighty deeds of God shift from Mary to the more general category of the *anawim* as a group. The greatness of the Lord is evident by his responding to the needs of the poor and his rejection of those who are arrogant and self-sufficient. The Gospel and the call to discipleship are not grounded in wealth, power, or intellectual certitude. Salvation is for *all* peoples (*each* generation in *every* land). All who open their hearts to the gift of Jesus are highly favored. When Jesus began to preach the Kingdom, it is the rejected who hear his voice. It is the *anawim* who recognized Jesus as the Savior.

The birth of Jesus did not bring to an end the *anawim*, the "poor ones" of Yahweh. For the *anawim* continue in history as a physical reminder of the greatness of the Lord. It is the remnant, these "poor ones," who witness to the blessings of salvation by the Lord. It is not wealth, power, worldly status, or intellectual sophistication that reveals Jesus as Savior. Such comes from above and finds a dwelling in the hearts of those who totally depend on God and trust in his promises.

The example of Mary, the very essence of discipleship, calls us to be the *anawim* of today. Once again, the Lord who is faithful to every promise is about to visit his people again (Lk 1:55). Only in recognition of our poverty are we able to proclaim the Lord's greatness. Only in acceptance of our lowliness can the Lord lift us to high places. Only in humility can we be taught the truth that sets us free. Only in our weakness can the child in the crib be our strength.

PRAYER

O Lord, give us each day the joy of the
Holy Spirit.
Let us rejoice at the coming of our Savior;
your ultimate gift to us.
Prepare our hearts to receive the One
who takes away the sin of the world.
Let Mary's Magnificat become our
daily hymn to your greatness
and the splendor of your goodness to us.

Each day, Lord, let us be part of the
"poor ones" who count you alone
as their richness. Let us experience
the saving grace of your coming into
our hearts.

Lord, we need to be purified of our
arrogance and cleansed of our
pride. Too often we sit on mighty
thrones and take delight in our
power. We engage in self-glory
rather than your praise.
We try to live as if the crib
with its Savior holds no
hope and speaks no truth.
In so doing we find ourselves
empty and far from your presence.

During this Advent season, look down
on us in our need and fill us
with the peace of the Savior. Do your
mighty deeds in us so that
our being will proclaim your greatness.
Let your eternal mercy be in us.

Reflection Questions

1. In what specific ways have you experienced the greatness of the Lord's gifts to you? How have you known the joy of the Holy Spirit? Did you share the gifts and joy of the Lord with others? How?
2. In what ways have you been closed to God's mercy? How have you refused to be part of the *anawim*? What area(s) in your life keep you from proclaiming the greatness of the Lord: power, pride, arrogance, wealth, beauty, a belief in your own salvation apart from Jesus? In what concrete ways are you struggling to overcome these temptations?
3. How have you actively worked to bring Yahweh's care for the poor? How have you helped those who are poor in spiritual resources and are searching for God? How are the Scriptures, prayer, Penance, and Eucharist sources of spiritual renewal?

Fourth Sunday of Advent
(Luke 1:56)

Returned Home

There is a yearning deep within us for home. Perhaps this longing is as old as our banishment from Eden (Gn 3:24). Humankind throughout history has been looking for the way back home. We want to once again know that primordial innocence and security that once characterized our existence. We long to walk with Yahweh in the cool of evening-tide in paradise. Yet, we are denied such a return. The "cherubim and fiery revolving sword guard the way to the tree of life" (Gn 3:24). We must live east of Eden and resist the temptation to look backward to what might have been. Ours is a forward journey in time. Out of our past we go forward in faith toward the Kingdom. For the Bible and the Christian, time is of one reality. The future comes through our past into the present. Our today is the groundwork for tomorrow. Faith cannot be separated from hope. Love unites both in revealing the truth of our lives. We can accept all that is yesterday. We can courageously live all that is today. We can confidently anticipate tomorrow in the sure hope that is God's word.

The more we dwell on the desire for home the more we come to realize that our longing is not geographical but existential, not material but spiritual. For home is that spiritual state of peace which comes from being true to *who* we are. Home is that state of being truly ourselves. If home is where the heart is; and where our heart is, so is our treasure; then home is that treasure beyond price. For it is only when we are home that true peace is ours.

The temptation is to turn our earthly dwelling into a permanent residence. We try to lay foundations which prevent the journey of faith. We want to be comfortable and secure in earthen vessels. Our faith can become mere formal religion. Our celebrations sound like noisy assemblies instead of praise to the living God. The work of discipleship is reduced to a moralism which obeys the letter of the law but not its spirit which gives life. We constantly look for hitching-posts instead of those sign-posts which point us to our lasting home in heaven.

Remain and Return

Mary is the model of discipleship who carefully balances remaining and returning. Mary leaves in haste to be with Elizabeth in order to share her joy and supply her needs. The visitation is not a quick stopover in order to catch up on the latest gossip. Mary's visitation of Elizabeth is genuine service to one in need; and, as such, care is taken to make sure that Elizabeth is treated with dignity. No doubt because of her age, Elizabeth had special needs. No doubt she had to talk with Mary in order to better understand what has occurred. Mary also has news of her own to share about the child in her womb. All of this takes time. Mary must remain in order to give the necessary time for reflection to yield its fruits. Hence, we are told that "Mary remained with Elizabeth about three months" (Lk 1:56).

At the same time, Mary will not stay forever. Luke ends the episode of the visitation by saying that "Mary returned home" (Lk 1:56). Mary, in true Christian service, knows when it is time to leave. There comes a point when one's service ends. There are other needs in other places that require our attention. Mary must return home to prepare for the birth of her own child. She must be with Joseph during this important time. Elizabeth cannot become an end in herself. If that happens, than Mary is no longer serving the needs of Elizabeth but her own. True Christian service knows when to move on to other ministries.

Mary teaches us that no ministry, relationship, or need can ever become ultimate. There comes a time when we must let go, move on, and let the one in need grow beyond *our* service. Service aims at liberation and empowerment of the other. We cannot become fixated in our earthly projects. All our relationships must be understood in light of our ultimate relationship with Jesus. Again, the temptation is great to make our good work ultimately lasting. We can view our ministry as indispensable. We can let our faith settle into a comfortable attitude which ceases to challenge us to grow in faith. In effect, we can build homes for ourselves in place of that lasting home which is heaven.

Throughout the Gospels we see the call to be pilgrims in faith. Mary will return home only to leave for Bethlehem. John the Baptist will grow up in the home of Elizabeth and Zechariah only to leave for "the desert until that day when he made his public appearance in Israel" (Lk 1:80). Likewise, Jesus will be subject to Mary and Joseph until he is called to leave for his public ministry (Mt 4:12-17). Even the resurrected Lord returns to the Father with the promise of coming again (Acts 1:10-11). Upon his return, the Lord will gather the faithful for that final journey to that banquet without end. For now we press on to that "life" which means Christ (Ph 1:21).

Pilgrim People

One of the favorite images used by the Council Fathers at the Second Vatican Council was the Church as a "pilgrim people." Much in the Church had become too settled and closed. The dust of certainty had covered over the deep riches of a living Tradition. The Council Fathers felt the wind of the Spirit once again moving as the creative breath for new life. Many of the intellectual, spiritual, and liturgical "homes" we built, needed some remodeling. This is never easy nor without the messy debris of any relocation and reconstruction. Yet the Spirit continues to be with the Church as we move into the third millennium with hope.

Mary reminds us that no earthly home is forever. No structure is left unshaken by the mighty God who makes all things new. Every relationship and good work points beyond to the God who alone is good (Mk 10:18). For even the barren and the virgin bring forth new life. The lowly are looked upon with favor by God. The expectations of the learned and self-sufficient are confounded by God's wisdom. The poor hear the Gospel. The rich are sent away while the needy have every good gift poured into the hem of their garments. For nothing is impossible with God (Lk 1:37).

Prayer

O Lord, all our earthly days are time
toward home. For to rest in you
is our lasting hope and peace.
Yet you know that our powers for
the journey are weak. We become
attached to the homes we build
as if their foundations are lasting.

Turn us from our folly. Let us know you
as our sure foundation. For with
you is truth and life in abundance.
The homes we inhabit become idols
which do not give life.
Our homes become tombs; monuments
to our arrogance from which we do not
rise.

Our own pilgrim journey enlivens our faith.
Let us live each day fully to your glory,
and not as a way of escaping your holy will.
Help us to surrender each precious thing
to you for safekeeping. We are confident

that in your care all things work unto
good. You do infinitely more than we expect.

Lord, you left your home to pitch your tent
with us. Let your loving pilgrimage of salvation
lead us to our lasting home with you. With your
grace nothing is impossible.

Reflection Questions

1. In what ways do you resist change; especially change in the Church? Why? Which area(s) of Church life have caused you the most anxiety? Which changes have been most beneficial? Why?
2. Do you tend to hold onto a particular ministry without leaving room for change? Relationships? In what ways has the Holy Spirit challenged you to explore new areas of service and ministry in the Church? How did you respond? Would you do things differently? Why? Why not?
3. In what significant ways have you changed toward the living of your faith in recent times? What struggles did you experience as you ventured into new spiritual places? Did these struggles help you grow spiritually? How?

December 23rd

(Luke 2:8-20)

Treasures In the Heart

The balanced life is the ideal we all seek. From the great philosophers, to spiritual masters, to contemporary secular gurus, a common thread that connects their teachings is the need for balance. Virtue is found in the middle. The scales of work and play, feast and famine, amusement and seriousness must be kept level if integration is to be realized. The same golden mean is needed between action and contemplation, visitation and domestic responsibilities.

Yet, ours is an age of excess and deficiency. We eat too much and then crash the latest diet. We become workaholics to the degree that we even work at having fun. Leisure time is too often filled with frantic activity. We amuse ourselves to the death of our ability to sustain serious thought or reflective action. We have come to fear the boredom that drives us to be constantly on the go in search of new diversions. Entertainment and travel have become the industries of escape for a sensate culture which requires ever new and more powerful forms of stimulation.

The season of Advent can easily become imbalanced as the secular meaning swallows the spiritual truths of this holy time. It is easy to get caught up in a series of high-pressure activities while ignoring the need to be still and listen. Even within the churches, we can find our individual and community lives out of balance. We can become absorbed in various liturgical, educational, and social justice out-reach ministries which leave little room for prayer, reflection, and reading. When this short but intense season finally culminates with Christmas, there is an emptiness inside. Instead of feeling the joy of the Holy Spirit at the birth of the Messiah, we feel let down and find ourselves wondering, "is that all there is?" There is an inner fatigue that replaces the peace that was meant to be.

The example of Mary, the first disciple, is essential if we are to find our way to the crib, for Mary is both disciple and mother, woman of annunciation and visitation. She discloses that balance necessary for entering into the mystery of the birth of the Messiah. Mary is at once the disciple who makes haste to be with Elizabeth in her joy and need, while knowing when to return home (Lk 1:56).

The Shepherds

In the Gospel of Matthew, a star in the east leads the wise men to the crib in Bethlehem so they can worship the Child. In the Gospel of Luke, the wise men are replaced by the shepherds who receive the angelic hymn of praise along with the glad tidings that the Savior is born (Lk 2:8-14). The reaction of the shepherds is similar to that of the magi — "glorifying and praising God" (Lk 2:20). Also, the shepherds and the wise men drop out of the Scriptures never to return. Their part in the birth of the Messiah is complete. The magi return to their country (Mt 2:12), and the shepherds return to their fields and their own towns (Lk 2:18; 20).

While the shepherds are favored with an angelic announcement about the Savior, there is a lack of depth of understanding on their part. The shepherds operate on the surface of the revelation. They *heard* the message of the angels and went "over to Bethlehem in order to *see* this event which the Lord has made known to them" (Lk 2:15). The shepherds in the end return to the fields. They do not go out to the world to proclaim the good news. They are at the first stage of faith, a stage of simply repeating what was said and seen. The deeper apostolic tack of preaching the Gospel and teaching about Jesus will come later, for the ministry of evangelization does not begin and end with the crib but must include the public ministry perfected in the Paschal Mystery. Neither the shepherds or magi are up to such a task. What is needed is one who "treasured all these things and reflected on them in her heart" (Lk 2:19). We must turn to Mary.

Reflective Heart

The magi return home. The shepherds go back to their flocks. It is Mary alone who is left to reflect on and interpret the deeper meaning of the events that have just taken place. The Mary who left in haste to be with Elizabeth must now be reflective in order to gain the truth of what occurred. Without the ability to prayerfully ponder what God has done, the deeper meaning of these events will be lost. Mary once again shows the maturity of balancing visitation with reflection. Mary is *the* disciple of the Lord.

The meaning of everyday events are not always obvious. Only later do we come to see their meaning. More so with the mighty works of God. We don't grasp their meaning immediately but only see their truth and God's love at work *after* prayerful consideration. Many things have happened to Mary. Many words have been proclaimed about her child. Mary does not rush to a shallow interpretation. She must treasure all these events in her heart. Their deepest meaning will only be revealed to her later. Only after Jesus' earthly ministry and Paschal Mystery, Pentecost, and her Assumption into heaven, will Mary fully understand the events of the past nine months. Only after Mary is received into heaven at the Assumption will she come to fully comprehend what the heavenly host proclaimed years earlier to the shepherds: "To you this day there is born in the city of David a Savior who is Messiah and Lord" (Lk 2:11).

Luke never wants us to forget that Mary is the disciple as well as mother of Jesus. As disciple she follows Jesus. Hers is a walk of faith, for she does not fully understand the mighty events of God. However, this human limitation does not keep her from trusting completely in the Lord. Mary is servant, handmaid, disciple, and mother to the Son of God. Mary does not wait for blessed certitude and absolute clarity before making a commitment. In walking by faith, a walk which is *not* blind, Mary trusts the One who makes and keeps promises. The God who kept promises to "our fathers, promised Abraham and his descendants forever," is the same God who now gives his Word to Mary. It is the living Word that Mary treasures in her heart and gives to the world as its Savior.

Prayer

O Lord, we find ourselves busy with
many things. Too often we have
not chosen the better portion — your
Word made flesh.
We find ourselves out of balance.
We are in need of the Holy Spirit
to prepare our hearts for the Savior.

Give us your Holy Spirit, Lord,
so that we may know the true
meaning of this holy season.
Let us become inwardly quiet so that
your mighty deeds of salvation will
be reflected on in our hearts.
In imitation of Mary, let us treasure
all that takes place.

Lord, help me to be that faithful servant
of the Word who hears, sees, and
acts on your revelation.
Give us the grace to hold your words in
our hearts. Empower us to be daily
witnesses of your saving love. Use us to

lead others to hear, see, and act on
your word.

Lord, even though we don't fully understand
your mighty works, let us walk by
faith in the truth of your love. For you
keep your promises and never abandon us.

Reflection Questions

1. In what ways do you find yourself struggling to find balance in your spiritual life? Do you place more emphasis on the contemplative dimensions? The apostolic? How can you integrate both in your relationship with Jesus?
2. What specific concerns have kept you from treasuring the events of this holy season? How can you overcome these concerns? Do you find yourself uncomfortable with quiet prayer? Why?
3. Do you find the Scriptures a source of blessing for understanding God's mighty events? What keeps you from turning to Scripture for guidance — lack of time, confusion over the meaning of the Bible, lack of support from your spiritual community or parish?

December 24th
(John 19:25-27)

Behold Your Mother

Why culminate Advent with Mary at the foot of the cross rather than at the crib? The crib is not a culmination as much as a commencement. The crib which receives the Savior cannot be separated from the cross which will hold the Messiah as Suffering Servant (Mk 15:34). Advent and Lent, Christmas and Easter must be taken together if we are to understand the message to the shepherds by the heavenly host: "This day in David's city a Savior has been born to you, the Messiah and Lord" (Lk 2:11). This "tidings of great joy" must always be preserved from becoming pure sentimentality. The joy at the birth of the Messiah must be matured by the sober reality of Golgotha.

It is easy to allow the secular culture of Christmas-as-holiday to overshadow the truth of Christmas-as-holy-day. Yes the Infancy Narratives speak of the magi, shepherds, gifts, glad tidings, joy, and God's peace on earth. At the same time the Scriptures do not flinch from the hard reality of rejection, lack of room in the inn, swaddling clothes, the murderous designs of Herod, and the blood of the Holy Innocents which raised "a cry... Rachel bewailing her children; no comfort for her, since they are no more" (Mt 2:18). The message of the angels is often met with the world's hostility. The heavenly host declare God's peace while the world continues its ways of violence.

The birth of the Messiah must encompass both realities: God's peace and the nations which rebel. To only proclaim peace turns the message of the angels into a romantic, sentimental escape from the principalities and powers opposed to the Kingdom. To experience only the love of power blinds us to love's power to win the ultimate victory. Hence crib and cross join together as the sure foundation in hope of God's triumphant love. Mary is the model of such a victory in love, for she brings forth the Word of life at Bethlehem and receives the Word of life at Golgotha. In both, she is faithful to her vocation: "I am the servant of the Lord" (Lk 1:38).

Downfall and Rise of Mary

Luke's Gospel is characterized by its emphasis on God's grace, compassionate love for sinners, the importance of women in God's plan for salvation, and the Holy Spirit as the one who bestows joy. At the same time, Luke does not shy away from the controversy that the birth of Jesus brings. This is powerfully captured by Luke at the presentation of Jesus in the Temple in fulfillment of the Law of Moses (Lk 2:22-40).

At the presentation of Jesus in the Temple, we meet Simeon and Anna who represent the pious Jews who are awaiting the Messiah. They also represent the *anawim* who rely totally upon God for consolation. Simeon is promised he would not die before seeing the Messiah. When Jesus is presented by Mary and Joseph, Simeon receives the child with a hymn of praise to God. The Lord has kept his word to Simeon. In this child is the One who is "a revealing light to the Gentiles, and the glory of your people Israel" (Lk 2:29-32). Simeon can now go in peace because God has kept his promise. The hope expressed in Isaiah (a major figure around the crib) is now fulfilled: with this child God comforts his people (Is 52:9), brings light to the Gentiles (Is 49:6), and glory to Israel (Is 46:13). All of these salvation themes in Isaiah are *now* realized in the child Jesus. Once again, God's faithful love does not disappoint. Jew and Gentile alike will receive God's mercy in the covenant of universal salvation (Acts 28:28).

The reaction of Mary and Joseph to Simeon's words about Jesus is understandable: They "were marveling at what was being said about him" (Lk 2:33). And why not? Here is their son once again being proclaimed as the consolation of Israel and the light to the Gentiles. What greater could be said? Any parent would thrill to hear such a pronouncement, especially by the holy man Simeon. Yet, there is more to be said.

Simeon's words shift from canticle to oracle, from hymn of praise to sober words of judgment: "This child is destined to be the downfall and the rise of many in Israel, a sign that will be opposed — and you yourself shall be pierced with a sword — so that the thoughts of many hearts may be laid bare" (Lk 2:34-35). The Messiah comes for the salvation of all peoples. There are Jews and Gentiles who will accept and *reject* the Gospel. Jesus came unto his own, but they received him not. To those who accept him they "became children of God" (Jn 1:11-12). Jesus will be a "sign of contradiction" that will engender the hostility of the Jewish authorities. For Jesus has not come for peace but a sword. His public ministry will cause division even in the intimate setting of the family; father and son, mother and daughter will be divided over him (Lk 12:51-53).

Even though Mary is the first disciple and mother of Jesus, she is not spared the need for a decision: "And you yourself shall be pierced with a sword" (Lk 2:35). Mary will not only be the mother of Jesus because of her affirmation at the annunciation, she will be the mother of the new family formed by those who accept Jesus as the Messiah (Lk 8:19-21). The sword that will pierce her heart is a decisional sword. As such, it brings to light the inmost thoughts of a person in terms of accepting or rejecting Jesus. This decisional sword is not just for Mary but comes to all who hear Jesus. The inner thoughts of Mary are continually revealed as those of a true disciple; in fact, she is the model of the true disciple. The same decisional sword will reveal the inner hostile thoughts of those who oppose Jesus such as the Pharisees (Lk 12:1-2).

For Luke, hostility and rejection *will not* have the final word. Also, in the Temple is "a certain prophetess, Anna by name" (Lk

2:36). She is a widow who is constantly praying and fasting in the Temple. Anna is a representative of the *anawim* (poor ones) who hope completely in the promises of the Lord. She recognizes Jesus and "talked about the child to all who looked forward to the deliverance of Jerusalem" (Lk 2:38). Anna's prophecy about the child indicates that God's plan for salvation will not be defeated by the violence of the world or even the rejection of Israel. To all, Jew and Gentile alike, Jesus brings consolation and salvation. But all that is in the future. For now the Holy Family returns to Nazareth. Jesus for his part "grew in size and strength, filled with wisdom, and the grace of God was upon him" (Lk 2:40).

Behold Your Son

At the crib, Mary pondered what was said about her son and treasured these things in her heart. It is at the foot of the cross that Mary comes to understand, in the deepest of ways, the mission of the Son who "must be about my Father's business" (Lk 2:49). The work of salvation comes at a dear price — death on the cross. It is from the cross that the new family of God is born. The Beloved Disciple is now the son of Mary. Mary is now the mother of the disciple whom Jesus loved (Jn 19:26-27). In the shadow of the cross, a new Holy Family comes into being.

On this eve of Christmas, let us ponder its meaning and treasure these things in our hearts.

Prayer

O Lord, the time of your birth is near.
On this holy night, let us become
inwardly silent in preparation for
your coming.

Let us quiet the noise of the world;
keep our hearts still so that we
too might hear the angels on high.
Help us to look at the crib and also
see the cross. Both are revelations
of your love. Both tell us the depth
of that love.

You did not love us in an abstract
way. You became our flesh. You
died our death. In your Resurrection
we have the hope of eternal life.

Lord, let us be one in hope with Isaiah;
let us be of courage like the Baptist;
a people of integrity in imitation of
Joseph; and always a servant of the
Word in following the example of Mary.

God, if we can open our hearts to these
graces we shall draw around the
crib of your Son and our Savior.
Send your Holy Spirit within us,
for the night will give way to the dawn.

In the space provided write your prayer in anticipation of the birth of Jesus.

Prayer

"Therefore the Lord himself will give you
this sign: the virgin shall be with
child, and bear a son, and shall name
him Emmanuel." (Isaiah 7:14)

"I baptize you in water for the sake
of reform, but the one who will follow
me is more powerful than I am." (Matthew 3:11)

"When Joseph awoke he did as the angel
of the Lord had directed him and
received her into his home as his wife."
(Matthew 1:24)

"Simeon blessed them and said to Mary
his mother: 'and you yourself
shall be pierced with a sword so that
the thoughts of many hearts may be
laid bare.'" (Luke 2:34-35)

"The Word became flesh… filled with
enduring love… of his fullness
we all have a share
love following upon love." (John 1:14;16)

Christmas
(Luke 2:12)

"...you will find an infant in swaddling clothes."

We human beings are awash in sign and symbol. From the traffic light to bread and wine, there is more about reality than we can say. We turn to the poet, artist, sage, and seer for those deeper glimpses into the really Real. And each of these turn to sign and symbol, to language and the stuff of everydayness to reveal the splendor that is all around. With each revelation we come to understand that life is a mystery rather than a problem to be solved (Marcel).

The mystery of the Incarnation lies before us. We find ourselves around the crib. Each of our Advent figures has played a part. From the dramatic call to Isaiah to the quiet strength of Joseph, from the courageous herald in the wilderness to the virgin who treasured all these things in her heart, our figures around the crib have made straight our path to Bethlehem. The prophet, herald, dreamer, and virgin have helped to draw us deeper into the mystery of God's unbounded love.

Now that we have arrived, we must do our part if the truth of this day is to be ours. Specifically, we are called to hear, to see, and to ponder all that God has done. Our Advent figures have given us an example; happy will we be if we live what they taught.

To Hear

The lyrics of a popular song from the movie *Midnight Cowboy* go something like this: "Everybody's talkin' at me. I don't hear a word they're sayin'; only the echo of my mind." It seems as if contemporary life is having everybody talking at us. From talk radio, to talk TV, to the countless chattering that fills the day, we seem to have little time for listening. Silence is a rare experience. Yet, if we are to enter the mystery of Christmas, we must know how to listen, not merely with our ear but with our heart.

The shepherds were able to hear the message of the angel concerning the birth of the Savior. No doubt, they were paying careful attention to their flocks. Someone might try to steal the sheep. An animal might be on the prowl for a meal. A sudden noise could panic the sheep causing them to scatter. Vigilance is essential for the good shepherd. Even with their focus on the flocks, they were able to hear the angel. The heavenly host joined in to proclaim, "Glory to God in the highest; peace on earth to those on whom his favor rests" (Lk 2:14).

With so much talk, so much "sound and fury" signifying little, the attentive heart is crucial. The message of the angel and heavenly host is the fulfillment of history and our heart's deepest longing — the gift of the Savior. It is so easy to be absorbed in the background noise and elevator music of this world. None of this is a call to withdraw from our daily responsibilities. The shepherds tended their sheep. The angel comes with the message of the Savior *while* they are tending the sheep. Likewise, in the midst of our everydayness, the message of salvation comes to us. It is a message that requires a listening heart.

To See

Revelation is not only for the ear; it is also for the eye. Not only must we hear with the heart, we must see with the eye of faith. The angel proclaims the birth of the Messiah along with a sign. The shepherds must not only hear the good news, they must *go and see*. If the Gospel remains only for the hearing, then it becomes lifeless, an intellectual abstraction which never touches us at our deepest level of existence. The Gospel becomes something we hear and then promptly go off and forget. The message must be joined with a sign; the listening heart must connect with the eye of faith.

What is the sign to be given? "Let this be a sign to you: in a manger you will find an infant wrapped in swaddling clothes" (Lk 2:12). Signs do not explain themselves, nor do signs point to themselves. The nature of signs is that they point *beyond* themselves to truths which go deeper than the surface meaning or conventional wisdom. Signs challenge our expectations and open up the possibilities to new ways of thinking, believing, and living. The sign of a child, in a manger, in swaddling clothes certainly challenges our expectation of Messiah and Savior. There is a deeper truth beyond the conventional hopes of the time. It is not even enough to hear; we must also see. It is not enough to engage the listening heart and focus the eye of faith; we must follow the way of Mary. We must *ponder* the words of the angel and the sign of the child in a manger wrapped in swaddling clothes. We too must let all this become a treasure in our hearts.

To Ponder

More is required of the true disciple of Jesus then merely hearing and repeating the Gospel. Mary is the model of discipleship because she goes beyond the shepherds. Mary ponders the *meaning* of what is said and what she observes. There are no easy or quick answers. To ponder the meaning of Jesus takes a lifetime and beyond. It is only after Pentecost and her Assumption into heaven that Mary's knowledge will be complete. Each episode in the life of Jesus deepened her understanding of what was spoken to her at the Annunciation. Throughout her life she continued to trust "that the Lord's words to her would be fulfilled" (Lk 1:45). Mary never demanded to understand everything all at once. As life unfolded, she was able to grow into that adventure of faith which leads to the One who is Love without end.

So it is with us on this Christmas Day. We have heard the

Gospel. We have seen the crib. It is now for us to ponder the meaning of what God has done. To be sure, we must be attentive with a listening heart in the midst of a noisy world. The eye of faith must see the truth of the crib and the One wrapped in swaddling clothes. In the midst of the world, we must dare to be active contemplatives. Within the routines of family, school, work, friendships, struggles, freedom, bondage, and all that life brings, there is the sign of the Child in the crib. The truth of our lives, and all existence, finds its expression with the Child in the crib. There is the truth that sets us free. And what is this truth?

The Child in the crib is the supreme example of the Law of the Gift. At the center of existence is Love as selfless donation. From the moment of creation; through the rebellion of sin and the promise of the Messiah; to the coming of Jesus; and to the time when he comes again in glory; the Law of the Gift is supreme. For it is only in that "love following upon love" that life is bearable and redemption possible (Jn 1:16). Time and again God empties himself and takes "the form of a slave, being born in the likeness of men" (Ph 2:7). It is only in the sign of such an emptying made visible in the crib, that the truth of our existence is understood.

Our "attitude must be that of Christ" (Ph 2:5). As we approach the crib, we must make our way inside and be drawn into the mystery of God's favor. We must lay aside the fine garments of self-sufficiency and vest ourselves in the swaddling clothes of "poor ones." In daily dying to ourselves, we are born anew in the name of the One who is Lord and Life (Ph 2:11).

We are given a lifetime to ponder these treasures of the heart. Now is the acceptable time. Around the crib is the appropriate place.

This book was designed and published by St. Pauls/ Alba House, the publishing arm of the Society of St. Paul, an international religious congregation of priests and brothers dedicated to serving the Church through the communications media. For information regarding this and associated ministries of the Pauline Family of Congregations, write to the Vocation Director, Society of St. Paul, 7050 Pinehurst, Dearborn, Michigan 48126. Phone (313) 582-3798 or check our internet site, www.albahouse.org